The World Intellectual Property Organization

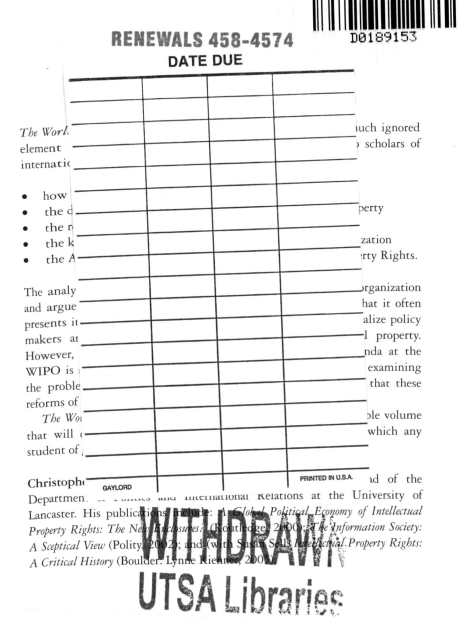

The World   luch ignored
element   scholars of
internatic

- how
- the d   perty
- the n
- the k   zation
- the A   rty Rights.

The analy   organization
and argue   hat it often
presents it   alize policy
makers ar   l property.
However,   nda at the
WIPO is   examining
the proble   that these
reforms of
   The Wo   ble volume
that will   which any
student of

Christophe   ad of the
Departmen... ... ...   International Relations at the University of
Lancaster. His publications include: *A Global Political Economy of Intellectual
Property Rights: The New Enclosures?* (Routledge, 2000); *The Information Society:
A Sceptical View* (Polity, 2002); and (with Susan Sell) *Intellectual Property Rights:
A Critical History* (Boulder: Lynne Rienner, 2005).

Routledge Global Institutions

Edited by Thomas G. Weiss
(The CUNY Graduate Center, New York, USA) and
Rorden Wilkinson
(University of Manchester, UK)

The "Global Institutions Series" is edited by Thomas G. Weiss (The CUNY Graduate Center, New York, USA) and Rorden Wilkinson (University of Manchester, UK) and designed to provide readers with comprehensive, accessible, and informative guides to the history, structure, and activities of key international organizations. Every volume stands on its own as a thorough and insightful treatment of a particular topic, but the series as a whole contributes to a coherent and complementary portrait of the phenomenon of global institutions at the dawn of the millennium.

Each book is written by a recognized expert in the field, conforms to a similar structure, and covers a range of themes and debates common to the series. These areas of shared concern include the general purpose and rationale for organizations, developments over time, membership, structure, decision-making procedures, and key functions. Moreover, the current debates are placed in an historical perspective alongside informed analysis and critique. Each book also contains an annotated bibliography and guide to electronic information as well as any annexes appropriate to the subject matter at hand.

The volumes currently published or under contract include:

The United Nations and Human Rights
A Guide for a New Era (2005)
by Julie A. Mertus (American University)

The UN Secretary-General and Secretariat (2005)
by Leon Gordenker (Princeton University)

United Nations Global Conferences (2005)
by Michael G. Schechter (Michigan State University)

The UN General Assembly (2005)
by M.J. Peterson (University of Massachusetts, Amherst)

The Organization for Security and Co-operation in Europe
by David J. Galbreath (University of Aberdeen)

UNHCR
The Politics and Practice of Refugee Protection Into the Twenty First Century
by Gil Loescher (University of Oxford), James Milner (University of Oxford), and Alexander Betts (University of Oxford)

The World Health Organization
by Kelley Lee (London School of Hygiene and Tropical Medicine)

The World Trade Organization
by Bernard Hoekman (World Bank) and Petros Mavroidis (Columbia University)

The International Organization for Standardization and the Global Economy
Setting Standards
by Craig Murphy (Wellesley College) and JoAnne Yates (Massachusetts Institute of Technology)

The International Olympic Committee
by Jean-Loup Chappelet (IDHEAP Swiss Graduate School of Public Administration) and Brenda Kübler-MabbottBank)

For further information regarding the series, please contact:

Craig Fowlie, Publisher, Politics & International Studies
Taylor & Francis
2 Park Square, Milton Park, Abingdon
Oxford OX14 4RN, UK

+44 (0)207 842 2057 Tel
+44 (0)207 842 2302 Fax

craig.fowlie@tandf.co.uk
www.routledge.com

The World Intellectual Property Organization

Organization
Resurgence and the Development Agenda

Christopher May

Routledge
Taylor & Francis Group

LONDON AND NEW YORK

First published 2007 by Routledge
2 Park Square, Milton Park, Abingdon, Oxon OX14 4RN

Simultaneously published in the USA and Canada
by Routledge
270 Madison Ave, New York, NY 10016

Routledge is an imprint of the Taylor & Francis Group, an informa business

© 2007 Christopher May

Typeset in Times New Roman by Taylor & Francis Books
Printed and bound in Great Britain by TJ International Ltd, Padstow, Cornwall

British Library Cataloguing in Publication Data
A catalogue record for this book is available from the British Library

Library of Congress Cataloging in Publication Data
A catalog record for this book has been requested

ISBN10: 0-415-35800-0   ISBN13: 978-0-415-35800-2 (hbk)
ISBN10: 0-415-35801-9   ISBN13: 978-0-415-35801-9 (pbk)
ISBN10: 0-203-00406-X   ISBN13: 978-0-203-00406-7 (ebk)

For Hilary

Contents

Foreword

The current volume is the eighth in a new and dynamic series on "global institutions." The series strives (and, based on the initial volumes we believe, succeeds) to provide readers with definitive guides to the most visible aspects of what we know as "global governance". Remarkable as it may seem, there exist relatively few books that offer in-depth treatments of prominent global bodies and processes, much less an entire series of concise and complementary volumes. Those that do exist are either out of date, inaccessible to the non-specialist reader, or seek to develop a specialized understanding of particular aspects of an institution or process rather than offer an overall account of its functioning. Similarly, existing books have often been written in highly technical language or have been crafted "in-house" and are notoriously self-serving and narrow.

The advent of electronic media has helped by making information, documents, and resolutions of international organizations more widely available, but it has also complicated matters. The growing reliance on the Internet and other electronic methods of finding information about key international organizations and processes has served, ironically, to limit the educational materials to which most readers have ready access – namely, books. Public relations documents, raw data, and loosely refereed websites do not make for intelligent analysis. Official publications compete with a vast amount of electronically available information, much of which is suspect because of its ideological or self-promoting slant. Paradoxically, the growing range of purportedly independent websites offering analyses of the activities of particular organizations have emerged, but one inadvertent consequence has been to frustrate access to basic, authoritative, critical, and well-researched texts. The market for such has actually been reduced by the ready availability of varying quality electronic materials.

For those of us who teach, research, and practice in the area, this access to information has been at best frustrating. We were delighted, then, when Routledge saw the value of a series that bucks this trend and provides key reference points to the most significant global institutions. They are betting that serious students and professionals will want serious analyses. We have assembled a first-rate line-up of authors to address that market. Our intention, then, is to provide one-stop shopping for all readers – students (both undergraduate and postgraduate), interested negotiators, diplomats, practitioners from non-governmental and intergovernmental organizations, and interested parties alike – seeking information about the most prominent institutional aspects of global governance.

The World Intellectual Property Organization: Resurgence and the Development Agenda

The World Intellectual Property Organization (WIPO) is something of a curiosity among global institutions. Although WIPO is frequently mentioned in the scholarly and policy literatures, few works actually explain what the organization does. Given the increasing importance, and indeed contentious nature, of intellectual property issues in world politics, our aim from the outset was to ensure that the series would include a book dealing with the principal institution in this area. We were delighted when Chris May agreed to write this text for us. His intellectual industry has been key to raising the profile of intellectual property as an issue for political scientists. His *Global Political Economy of Intellectual Property Rights* remains one of the most important contributions in the field.[1] We have no doubt that his book on WIPO will also be a major success and, more importantly, one that becomes required reading for all interested in global institutions.

What follows is an accessible, critical, and authoritative account of WIPO. Throughout the book, May shows that WIPO's story is about more than just its involvement in the steady globalization of intellectual property protection. As an institution, WIPO has demonstrated a degree of institutional longevity, resilience, and dynamism exuded by few other organizations.[2] Although comparatively young in international organizational terms – only established in 1970 – its roots are in moves to protect intellectual property during the industrial expansion of the nineteenth century under the 1883 Paris Convention for the Protection of Industrial Property and the 1886 Berne Convention for the Protection of Literary and Artistic Works.[3] These too are part of May's story.

Yet, as he also shows, this historical antecedence and institutional longevity has not protected WIPO from significant challenges to its role as the main institutional focus for intellectual property rights protection. May documents how the U.S. and European pursuit of greater intellectual property right enforcement during the 1970s and 1980s and its realization in the World Trade Organization's (WTO) Agreement on Trade Related Intellectual Property Rights (TRIPs) not only raised questions about WIPO's continued relevance but also reinvigorated it to meet this challenge.

This is an excellent book. It is invaluable reading not only for those interested in intellectual property and its regulation but also for those seeking to better understand systems of global governance. We are pleased to recommend it to all. As always, comments and suggestions from readers are welcome.

Thomas G. Weiss, The CUNY Graduate Center, New York, USA
Rorden Wilkinson, University of Manchester, UK
September 2006

Acknowledgements

This book was prompted partly by the realization that of all the specialized agencies of the United Nations, and other international governmental organizations, the World Intellectual Property Organization is more often alluded to, or listed, in studies of the international political economy or global governance, than discussed in any great detail. I am grateful to the editors of this series, and specifically Rorden Wilkinson for suggesting that I should rectify this lacuna. As I have done before, I would like to acknowledge the continuing influence of my late father, John May, whose diligence and hard work (albeit in a different vocation) remain an example for my own practices. My work on intellectual property over the years has also been greatly influenced by the joint history project that Professor Susan Sell and I worked on for over half a decade, now published by Lynne Rienner Publishers as *Intellectual Property Rights: A Critical History* (2005). Susan has been a great friend, supporter and a wonderful co-author; her influence is suffused throughout the following chapters. More specifically, as regards the WIPO, I was greatly helped by Deborah Halbert who very kindly shared with me a substantial amount of material generated by her visit to the WIPO in Geneva in summer 2005. This book has also been greatly influenced through its gestation by the comments and advice of Geoff Tansey, and the work of Sisule Musungu and Graham Dutfield, and of William New and his colleagues at *IP Watch*; I hope that I have done their efforts justice.

While writing this volume I have moved institutions: I would like to take this chance to thank my colleagues in the School of Politics at the University of the West of England for supporting my research, of which this volume is merely the latest installment. Specifically, I gratefully acknowledge the support and friendship of: Dean McSweeney, Nick Buttle, Dimitrios Christopolous, Peter Clegg, Alan Greer, Lisa Harison and Jamie Munn, as well as Geoff Channon, June

Hannam, John Hatt and Jem Thomas. At my new home, the Department of Politics and International Relations, Lancaster University, I would like to acknowledge the support and encouragement I have already received from David Denver, Gideon Baker, Feargal Cochrane, Bob Jessop, Sol Piciotto, David Sugarman, and Cindy Weber. Lastly, but most importantly, I could not continue with my work (or my life more generally) without enjoying the love of my wife, Hilary Jagger, to whom I have been married for twenty years; she is the person who keeps me sane and allows me my little foibles, and it is to her that I dedicate this book.

List of Abbreviations

BIRPI	*Bureaux Internationaux réunis pour la protection de la propriété intellectuelle*
DRM	digital rights management
GIPID	Global Intellectual Property Issues Division
GSP	General System of Preferences
ICANN	Internet Corporation for Assigned Names and Numbers
INGO	international non-governmental organization
IPC	Intellectual Property Committee
IPRs	intellectual property rights
OECD	Organization for Economic Cooperation and Development
PCT	Patent Cooperation Treaty
QUNO	Quaker United Nations Office
TRIPs	Trade Related Aspects of Intellectual Property Rights agreement
UN	United Nations
UNCTAD	United Nations Conference on Trade and Development
UNDP	United Nations Development Program
UNESCO	United Nations Education Scientific and Cultural Organization
UNIDO	United Nations Industrial Development Organization
USTR	Office of the United States Trade Representative
UDRP	Uniform Dispute Resolution Policy
WIPO	World Intellectual Property Organization
WTO	World Trade Organization

1 Intellectual Property

The World Intellectual Property Organization (WIPO) is one of the least discussed of the major international organizations in International Political Economy analyses. While sometimes mentioned in passing, most political economic analysis of the contemporary global system focuses on better known organizations such as the World Trade Organization (WTO) or the World Bank. For instance, critical treatments of global governance have little to say about the WIPO,[1] while Anne-Marie Slaughter only mentions the organization in passing in her influential discussion of international governmental networks.[2] Likewise more general treatments of the field sometimes mention the WIPO, but none have accorded the organization any extended attention.[3] Thus, since its establishment in 1970, and despite having been a specialized agency of the United Nations (UN) since 1974, international political economists have shown little interest in the WIPO.

This is all the more surprising as in the last decades, the political economy of intellectual property has moved from the margins to a much more central position in the study of global politics. The "problem" of intellectual property is no longer regarded as merely a technical issue of interest only to lawyers and specialist policy analysts. The relative inattention to the WIPO may reveal a tacit acceptance of its own public depiction of itself as merely a technical agency. However, the WIPO is a highly politicized organization whose role in the contemporary global political economy requires more thorough analytical attention.

Many commentators in the media and in universities have argued that the emergence of a "new economy," or a new "information age," has accorded such importance to the commodification of knowledge and information that it is hardly surprising that the political economy of intellectual property should be considered a more mainstream concern than it was perhaps twenty years ago. Although some of the claims for a wholesale social revolution should be discounted,[4] nevertheless there can be little doubt that the mechanisms for establishing property rights over intellectual resources are more widely recognized now than they were in the recent past. Furthermore, these technological shifts have produced a widespread concern about the extent of unauthorized copying of new digital products, most obviously in the music and software industries.[5] This concern has been expressed through high-profile campaigns against "piracy" and increasingly draconian punishments for infringers of intellectual property rights (IPRs).

Equally, high-profile disputes about access to AIDS-related medicines, and access to information over the Internet, as well as many people's personal experiences of the actions of copyright holders have encouraged political activists and academic analysts to recognize the importance of intellectual property. Throughout the world music lovers have been tempted to download music from the Internet, only to find that many of the early services such as Napster were actually illegal, while health activists have been outraged by the use of pharmaceutical patents to effectively restrict access to life-saving medicines. However, while these and other examples have encouraged a more forthright engagement with the WIPO in the global advocacy community, this has been much less evident in academic analysis.

One of the key reasons for the heightened profile of intellectual property in global politics is that since 1995 intellectual property rights have been subject to the Trade Related Aspects of Intellectual Property Rights (TRIPs) agreement overseen by the WTO. While this agreement does not completely determine national legislation regarding patents, copyrights, trademarks and other intellectual properties, for members of the WTO to be TRIPs-compliant their domestic intellectual property law must support the protections and rights that are laid out in TRIPs' 73 articles. The agreement represents an undertaking to uphold certain standards of protection for IPRs and to provide legal mechanisms for their enforcement. Perhaps most importantly, for the first time a multilateral trade treaty has required not merely changes in the manner in which imports and exports are regulated at national borders but has also required significant undertakings as regards national legislation for non-internationally traded products.

Prior to 1995, there were long-standing multilateral treaties in place regarding the international recognition and protection of intellectual property, overseen by the WIPO. Unfortunately, these were widely regarded as essentially toothless in the face of "piracy" and the frequent disregard for the protection of non-nationals' intellectual property outside the most developed countries, and even sometimes between them. The US government alongside its allies in the European Union believed that there were clear advantages to be gained by having a tougher multilateral enforcement mechanism. Additionally, linking IPR-related issues to the international trade regime by moving their regulation into the new WTO, at the expense of the WIPO's regulatory competence, US and EU negotiators felt that they were more likely to gain agreements to their advantage.[6] Subsequently the WIPO has struggled to re-establish its role in the increasingly global realm of intellectual property governance, and while not having regained its earlier policy dominance the organization has managed to remain intimately connected with the global governance of intellectual property.

One of the most interesting, yet under-analyzed issues in contemporary global governance is how the WIPO has fought long and hard to retain its position in the international regulation of IPRs. Moreover, despite the abundant evidence of the organization's clear political and normative agenda, the WIPO has also managed to maintain the external perception of it as merely a technical agency, and has thus been largely ignored even by the critics of contemporary global governance arrangements. This book is intended to reveal that this lack of attention is a serious shortfall in analytical attention. In other words, the WIPO, like other elements of the current regime of global governance, is highly politicized and must be (re)inserted into any account of global governance.

The origins of the WIPO itself can be traced back to the late nineteenth century and the discussions that established the first international conventions to govern the international trade in products covered by national patents and copyrights. Therefore, although only established in 1970 by a convention that had been signed in Stockholm three years earlier, the organization's history really commences with the 1883 Paris Convention for the Protection of Industrial Property, and the 1886 Berne Convention for the Protection of Literary and Artistic Works. Both conventions established secretariats and these were united in 1893 to form an organization that functioned under various names until it was formally consolidated in 1970 at the WIPO. The organization has a good claim to extensive experience, and considerable expertise built up over many years, in the international governance of intellectual property. It is this experience and expertise that has ensured that the WIPO has been able to avoid being completely side-stepped by the actions of major governments at the WTO.

In 2004 a number of developing country members of the WIPO, supported by a group of international non-governmental organizations (INGOs) sought to establish a more explicitly development-oriented policy agenda for the organization. This attempt to shift the WIPO's priorities is underpinned by the argument that as the WIPO is a specialized agency of the UN it should share the UN's focus on global developmental issues rather than a more technical focus on the governance and protection of IPRs. At the center of the Development Agenda is a critique of the WIPO that suggests it represents a narrowly focussed set of political economic interests that seek to expand the realm of commodified knowledge and information for their own commercial advantage. This book is intended to offer a context for such debates through an examination of the history of the organization, the way it works and its impact on the global governance of IPRs.

Within the study of global governance and more generally across the myriad disciplines of the social sciences that might have some interest in the questions around intellectual property, there sometimes seems to be some confusion about what exactly intellectual property and IPRs actually are. Therefore before examining the various aspects of the political economy of the WIPO it is as well to be clear, at least in a general sense, about the characteristics of IPRs.

A Brief Primer on Intellectual Property Rights: Forms and Functions

For purposes of clarity this section briefly sets out some of the basic issues for readers who are relatively new to the subject, and who may not be sure exactly what the various forms of intellectual property are. This section can easily be skipped by those who are already familiar with the characteristics, purposes and justifications entailed in making knowledge and information property.

What is intellectual property?

When knowledge becomes subject to ownership, IPRs express the legal benefits of ownership, most importantly: the ability to charge rent for use; to receive compensation for loss; and to gather payment for transfer. Intellectual property rights are sub-divided into a number of groups, of which two generate most discussion: industrial intellectual property (patents) and literary or artistic intellectual property (copyrights). Conventionally, the difference between patents and copyrights is presented as being between a patent's protection of an idea, and copyright's protection of the expression of an idea, and although this simple distinction has become increasingly difficult to draw for a number of reasons, it still holds some use as a starting point. Within the law of intellectual property, the balance between private rewards and the public interest in having relatively unrestricted access to knowledge and/or information has generally been traditionally expressed through time limits on IPRs, which is to say unlike material property, IPRs are formally only temporary rights. Once their time has expired the knowledge enters the public realm of freely available material that can be used without authorization by, or payment to, an owner.

For patents the knowledge which is to be registered and thus made property should be applicable in industry. To be patentable an idea must be:

* *new*, not already in the public domain or the subject of a previous patent;
* *non-obvious*, it should not be common-sense to any accomplished practitioner in the field who having been asked to solve a particular practical problem would see this solution immediately. This is to say, it should not be self-evident using available skills or technologies;
* *useful*, or *applicable in industry*, it must have a stated function, and could immediately be produced to fulfill this function.

For instance, a new device to drive nails into wood would be patentable, provided that it fulfilled the above criteria. However, something that was a discovery would not be; discoveries are not *new* as they existed prior to their discovery. Thus the fact that a heavier hammer will drive nails into wood more quickly is a product of the "natural" relationship between mass, acceleration and the exchange of energy; these are laws of nature and thus not amenable to patenting. The classic examples of such non-patentable items would be mathematical formulae or natural compounds. However, in both these cases, the former relating to computer software, the latter to biotechnology, there has been considerable debate about patents that seem to have awarded property rights over discoveries rather than inventions.

Nevertheless, in general, and following the harmonization of national legislation in the TRIPs agreement, if the above three conditions are fulfilled then an idea can be patented in any of the members of the WTO. The patent is lodged at the national or regional patent office, which for an agreed fee will allow others access to the patented knowledge as expressed in the patent document. Perhaps more importantly the office will also police and facilitate the punishment of unauthorized usage. Patents are an institutionalized bargain between the state and the inventor. The state agrees to ensure the inventor is paid for their idea when others use it, for the term of the patent, while the inventor allows the state to lodge the idea in its public records to facilitate wider dissemination of the advance.

Unlike patent, copyright is concerned with the form of knowledge and information that would normally be termed, "literary and artistic works." This is usually expressed in words, symbols, music, pictures, three-dimensional objects, or some combination of these different forms. Copyright therefore covers: literary works (fiction and non-fiction); musical works (of all sorts); artistic works (of two- *and* three-dimensional form and importantly irrespective of content – from "pure art" and advertising to amateur drawings and your child's doodles); maps; technical drawings; photography; audio-visual works (including cinematic works, video and forms of multi-media); and audio recordings. In some jurisdictions this may stretch to broadcasts and also typographical arrangements of publications. However, the underlying ideas, the plot, the conjunction of colors do not receive protection, only the specific expression attracts copyright.

Copyright is meant to ensure that what is protected should not be reproduced without the express permission of the creator (or the owner of the copyright, which may have been legally transferred to another party by the creator). This is often limited to an economic right, where the creator (or copyright owner) is legally entitled to a share of any return that is earned by the utilization or reproduction of the copyrighted knowledge. In some jurisdictions however, principally in continental Europe, there is an additional moral right not to have work tampered with or misrepresented. In all cases, failure to agree terms prior to the act of reproduction or duplication may result in any income being awarded to the original copyright holder by the court if an infringement is deemed to have taken place. Unlike patents however, copyright resides in the work from the moment of creation; all that is required is that the creator can prove that any supposed infringement is a reproduction of the original work, in terms of content, and that it was the product of an intended action of copying. Thus, for instance, the Verve, having used an unauthorized music sample, now pay all the royalties from their biggest hit single, "Bittersweet Symphony", to the Rolling Stones in settlement of a copyright court case.

Trademarks serve to distinguish the products of one company from another and can be made up of one or more distinctive words, letters, numbers, drawings or pictures, emblems or other graphic representations. Generally trademarks need to be registered, and in the act of registration a check is carried out to ensure that there are no other companies currently registering the same word, symbol or other representation as a trademark in the sector of the economy nominated by the registering company. A history of use of a trademark may establish its viability and support its subsequent legal recognition. Thus, a particular trademark is unlikely to succeed in being registered if it is too similar to, or liable to cause confusion with, a trademark already registered by another company (referred to as "passing off"). Neither will it be able to enjoy protection if the term or symbol is already in common use. In some jurisdictions the outward manifestation of packaging, provided that it is not a form necessarily dictated by function, may also be subject to trademark status (of which the most famous case is the Coke bottle).

There are other sorts of intellectual property, from process patents (which are like patents but cover processes as opposed to actual machines) to geographical indicators (such as "champagne"), but these share the key characteristics noted above; they code a form of information or knowledge as ownable property. However, in the case of geographical indicators this is more like a collective trademark: the indicator is limited in use to a defined group using a specified process, traditional to, or identified with, a specific locale. No-one "owns" a geographical indicator as such, but those that benefit from its recognition can seek protection from those outside the area trying to "pass off" their products as the same as those produced in the area. For instance, recent disputes have involved the processes that make ham "Parma ham," and what exactly makes a Melton Mowbray pie distinctive. Geographical indicators, as this suggests, are often although not exclusively concerned with food and drink markets.

It is sometimes also useful to think of trade secrets as intellectual property. Although a form which is not made public, trade secrets allow the control or ownership of knowledge. In one way the trade secret is the ultimate private knowledge property. However, while in some celebrated cases a trade secret is relied on to maintain a competitive advantage (and again the example of Coke is apposite, along with Kentucky Fried Chicken's "secret blend of herbs and spices"), in the main those who rely on knowledge as a resource adopt an intellectual property approach to protection, rather than keeping such knowledge completely secret. Indeed, for the knowledge industries it would be counter-productive, impossible even, to function on the basis of knowledge being secret, given the importance of reproduction and transfer of that knowledge to generate income and profit.

Intellectual property constructs a balance between public availability and private benefit which allows wider access to knowledge and information than trade secrecy. However, this availability is only within specific legal limits constructed by intellectual property. Indeed, where governments have recognized that despite the legal system imposed, this balance is not well served by specific IPRs being recognized, they have intervened to compulsorily license the invention or process or product for the wider social good. This state appropriation of property has historically usually only been used in extreme circumstances, but has remained a potential policy intervention, for patents especially, in most jurisdictions. The question of compulsory license remains highly contentious, as the debates about the use of generic substitutes for patented AIDS drugs in the developing world reveal.

Why is intellectual property needed?

Most importantly, while they remain active (that is, while they are within their time limits), IPRs formally construct scarcity of use where none necessarily exists. Knowledge and information, unlike material things, are not necessarily rivalrous; co-incident usage seldom detracts from utility. Most of the time knowledge, before it is made into property, does not exhibit the characteristics of material things. Take the example of a hammer as material property; if I own a hammer and you and I would both like to use it, our utility is compromised by sharing use. I cannot use the hammer while you are, you cannot while I am, our intended use is rival. Thus, for you to also use my hammer, either you have to accept a compromised utility, relying on my goodwill to allow you to use it when I am not, or you must buy another hammer. The hammer is scarce. However, the idea of building something with hammer and nails is not scarce. If I instruct you in the art of simple construction, once that knowledge has been imparted, your use of that information has no effect on my own ability to use the knowledge at the same time, there is no compromise to my utility. We may be fighting over whose turn it is to use the hammer, but we do not have to argue over whose turn it is to use the idea of hammering a nail into a joint; our use of the idea of cabinet construction is non-rival. Ideas, knowledge and information are generally non-rivalrous.

To be sure, if you and I were both cabinet makers, then instructing you in cabinet construction might lead you to compete for my customers, possibly reducing my income. But this might also lead us to say that any secrecy regarding my skills was anti-competitive. There are also other cases where knowledge may produce advantages for the holder, by enabling a better price to be extracted, or by allowing a market advantage to be gained; these are called information asymmetries. Here information and knowledge *is* rivalrous, and wider availability of this knowledge would cause market advantage to be compromised. However, rivalrousness is not necessarily of any wider social benefit: competition is often beneficial to customers, while information asymmetries produce market choices that are not fully informed and which therefore can be harmful.

When information is "naturally" rivalrous, the social good may be best served by ensuring that it is shared not hoarded. For instance, many problems for buyers in the second-hand car market could be ameliorated if car dealers were required to reveal *all* they knew about the cars they were selling. This would likely reduce the price they could obtain for much of their stock, but would enhance the general satisfaction (and even safety) of second-hand car buyers. Conversely, if trademarks offer useful information regarding the origin, reputation and quality of goods and services, then allowing anyone to use specific marks reduces their social utility as the information they impart becomes less reliable. Here the imposed scarcity *does* serve a wider social purpose, while also benefiting the owner of the mark who can treat it as a commercial asset; well-known trademarks are often accorded significant monetary value by companies and their shareholders.

To sum up: it is difficult to extract a price for the use of non-rival knowledge-related goods, so a legal form of scarcity that we call intellectual property is introduced to ensure a price can be obtained for use. Material property is "naturally" scarce and therefore already rival in potential use, whereas knowledge in most cases is non-rival prior to becoming intellectual property. Therefore, as Arnold Plant stressed seventy years ago, unlike "real" property rights, patents and other IPRs

> are not a *consequence* of scarcity. They are the deliberate creation of statute law; and, whereas in general the institution of private property makes for the preservation of scarce goods, tending (as we might somewhat loosely say) to lead us "to make the most of them," property rights in patents and copyright make possible the *creation* of scarcity of the products appropriated which could not otherwise be maintained. Whereas we might expect the public

action concerning private property would normally be directed at the prevention of the raising of prices, in these cases the object of the legislation is to confer the power of raising prices by enabling the creation of scarcity.[7]

The protection of rights for the express purpose of raising prices is, of course, the central issue that the political economy of intellectual property has to deal with. This means that significant political effort has been put in over the years to justify and legitimize the making of property from knowledge and information.

How is property in knowledge usually justified?

In contemporary debates about IPRs the assertion that there is a clear metaphorical link, indeed a workable similarity between property in material objects and property in knowledge, information or intellectual creations, is maintained as unproblematic. Here I will summarize the three main narratives used to justify intellectual property based on this metaphorical relationship, which I have explored at greater length elsewhere.[8] Not only commentators but also legal documents and judgements, sometimes explicitly, but more often implicitly, draw on these material property-related narratives to justify the recognition of property in knowledge. These justifications are used in the TRIPs agreement and have been mobilized in the cases brought to the WTO's dispute settlement mechanism, as well as being evident across all of the WIPO's documents and activities, most importantly including their training programs. Therefore they play a profound and important role in the way the global regime of protection of IPRs is both governed and reproduced.

The first narrative argues for labor's desert: the effort that is put into the improvement of nature requires it should be rewarded. In John Locke's influential formulation this was modeled on the improvement of land.[9] The application of effort to produce crops and/or improved resource yields justified the ownership of specific tracts of land by whoever worked to produce such improvement. Starting from this initial position Locke then argued there was also a right in disposal, mediated by money. This led him to conclude that all property, even after its initial sale or transfer, could be justified on the basis it had originally been produced through the labor of an individual. More importantly, property was also justified because it encouraged the improvement of nature through the reward of effort. Therefore the Lockean argument supports property by suggesting property encourages individual effort through the reward of ownership of the fruits of work. In contemporary debates around intellectual property the argument that patents and other intellectual properties reward the effort which has been put into their development has become a commonplace, with the research investment made to develop a patented innovation and the marketing expense in establishing a trademark two common examples.

However, sometimes this argument is supported through the mobilization of another, secondary story; the notion of property's links with the self as originally proposed by Georg Hegel.[10] Here the control and ownership of property is a significant part of the (re)production of selfhood, inasmuch as selfhood relates to the establishment of individual social existence. It is the manner in which individuals protect themselves from the invasions and attacks of others. For Hegel, the state legislates for property as part of its bargain with civil society. Individuals allow the state to operate in certain areas but protect their individuality and sovereignty through the limitations that property rights put upon the state vis-à-vis the individual's own life and possessions. In intellectual property law on the European continent this supports the inalienable moral rights that creators retain over their copyrights even after their formal transfer to new owners. In Anglo-Saxon law this narrative has been less well received due to its implications for the final alienability of intellectual property. Nonetheless, especially where "passing off" of trademarks (the unauthorized use of logos and brand names, often on substandard goods), and the pirating of copyrighted material (the downloading of music, for instance) are concerned, this justificatory narrative can sometimes be noted in the calls for redress based on the diminution of reputation, or the ownership of (self) expression.

There is a third narrative of justification which often underpins the role of intellectual property. In this pragmatic or economic argument the emergence of property rights is presented as a response to the needs of individuals wishing to allocate resources among themselves.[11] Thus, Douglass North argues the enjoyment of benefits, as well as the assumption of costs, takes place in social relations through the mobilization of useful resources. The institution of property arose to ensure that such resources have attached to them the benefits, and the costs that accrue to their use, and this increases "efficiency."[12] In this story property rights took the place of social trust-based relations, and allowed complex trade relations to form over distance where interpersonal links were less developed.

Mobilizing a history of material property, this third story suggests that efficient resource use is established through the use of markets in which property is exchanged and transferred to those who can make best use of it. The development of modern economies is predicated therefore on the institution of property, and its ability to ensure the efficient use of limited resources. In this justification, it is this efficiency requirement that drives the historical development of property rights, and now underpins the commodification of knowledge. This institutionalist (re)telling of the history of property carries with it the notion that property arose to ensure the efficient allocation of scarce economic resources. Even when it is accepted that this allocation may not be "optimal," property rights are still presented as the most efficient method of allocation available, even though they often produce a less than perfect solution. In the interests of "efficiency," property as an institution is reproduced through its legal and social use. This narrative of the efficient allocation of scarce resources is then brought to bear on the allocation and use of knowledge by any number of industries and corporations.

As a subset of this third justification that is also linked to the first, one of the most common arguments utilized to substantiate IPRs is the need to support innovation. Drawing from Locke the notion of reward for effort in improvement, and from the third narrative the idea of social efficiency, it is often asserted that without IPRs there would be little stimulus for innovation. Why would anyone work towards a new invention, a new solution to a problem, if they were unable to profit from its social deployment? Thus, not only does intellectual property reward intellectual effort, it actually stimulates activities that have a social value, and therefore serves to support the social good of progress. Underlying this argument is a clear perception of what drives human endeavor; individual benefit and reward. Only by encouraging and rewarding the individual creator or inventor with property rights in a creation or invention which leads to market-related benefits, can any society ensure that it will continue to develop important and socially valuable innovations, which will serve to make society as a whole more efficient.

These arguments or stories are often deployed subtly and in varying combinations, but the key issue is that because intellectual property by design changes the characteristics of knowledge and/or information, there needs to be some narrative of justification to help support the legitimization of this move. Hence, in disputes about IPRs, their recognition and their (global) governance, these arguments seldom lie far beneath the surface of any set of debates. Certainly these arguments can be persuasive, but equally they are seldom any longer accorded the status of being self-evidently true. Rather in the new millennium the realm of intellectual property has become widely contested and problematic. This is not to say any of these stories is without merit, only that they are of less widespread applicability than hard-line supporters of the extension of the protection of IPRs may suppose or hope.

These stories are also a major element of the normative arsenal of the WIPO, utilized in their technical assistance programs, and in the debates within the organization about the future trajectory of the global governance of intellectual property. One of the key roles that the WIPO has played in the last decade has been to introduce these stories to policy makers and legislators from the new developing country members of the WTO. Thus, not only does the organization fulfill a technical role, facilitating negotiation and the development of new legislative instruments by governments with little or no history in the regulation of IPRs, but perhaps more importantly, the WIPO acts as an agent of socialization. It is this less heralded and discussed function that will be the focus of much that follows.

Organization of the Book

In the next chapter the history of the WIPO is laid out from its origins with the 1883 Paris Convention, and the 1886 Berne Convention, through to its formal establishment as the WIPO in 1970, and its subsequently institutional link with the UN as a specialized agency. While the WIPO is a relatively young institution, being only thirty years old, it can trace its origins back into the nineteenth century and as such can be seen as a continuing reflection of the institutional dynamic that prompted a number of other sectoral organizations. Once the history of the WIPO has been set out, in chapter three we examine the manner in which the organization works. Broadly speaking, the WIPO currently fulfills three major roles in the realm of intellectual property:

1   It acts as a registrar and administrator for a number of international agreements, of which the Patent Cooperation Treaty (PCT) is the most important, not least of all as this activity generates most of the funds that allow the WIPO to remain largely independent of state funding;
2   it promotes and supports the adoption and expansion of intellectual property legislation throughout the developing world. It is this second element that has often been more contentious than the Director General and the staff of the WIPO would really like;
3   it is one of the key forums for discussions and policy development to extend the global governance of intellectual property beyond the minimum standards set by the TRIPs agreement.

The fourth chapter looks at three key issues, to help understand the manner in which the WIPO functions in the wider realm of the global governance of intellectual property. Using the example of the protection and enforcement of trademarks over the Internet, we examine the relationship between the WIPO and the Internet Corporation for Assigning Names and Numbers. This case has become widely discussed and allows us to see how the WIPO is able to influence areas beyond its formal oversight. The chapter then moves to examine the WIPO's extensive technical support and capacity building activities, another area of operations where the WIPO's international influence is extensive, before moving to examine its role in the further development and expansion of the regime of global governance for intellectual property. Having explored a number of key practices, the fifth chapter then explores the wide-ranging critique of the WIPO that has emerged from representatives and delegates of the developing country members of the organization, as well as some vocal non-governmental organizations. This discussion focuses on the recently proposed Development Agenda, and highlights the question of the WIPO's role as a specialized agency of the UN, before also assessing the WIPO's claim that it is merely a technical organization, remaining neutral in the global politics of IPRs.

The final chapter draws this discussion together to examine the sidelining and subsequent resurgence of the WIPO during the last twenty or so years, and concludes that the WIPO is an organization that has fought long and hard to retain its position in global governance. What is therefore interesting is the relative lack of consideration that the WIPO has received in various analytical accounts of the mechanisms of global governance. This book is itself meant to start to rectify this lacuna. Until recently, despite the abundant evidence of the organization's clear political and normative agenda, the WIPO has managed to maintain its (political) appearance as merely a technical agency. I hope that once you have read this book you will appreciate that this is a difficult case to make; rather the WIPO, like other elements of the current regime of global governance, is highly politicized.

2 The WIPO's Antecedents and History

The roots of the World Intellectual Property Organization stretch back into the nineteenth century. The organization's antecedents lie in the development of an international trade in products whose value rested, at least in part, on their knowledge or informational elements, and which were therefore subject to various forms of intellectual property rights (IPRs) in national markets. Indeed, prior to the last quarter of the nineteenth century the regulation of intellectual property was entirely a national issue,[1] with no formal framework for the international co-ordination of the recognition of rights over intellectual property.

In the 25 years between 1850 and 1875 an international controversy developed between those seeking to defend the protection of innovation and invention through the patent system, and those who contrasted this protection with the needs and demands of an international system of free trade.[2] Debates centered on the tension between free trade and intellectual property that stems from the limitations on commercial practice that the recognition of one party's IPRs puts on another party's activities, thereby limiting *free* trade. Free trade liberals criticized the monopoly aspect of intellectual property and tried to undermine the patent system by arguing that invention was social and a product of technological change, rather than the result of individual genius. Using examples of simultaneous invention, and looking at human innovation prior to any national patenting system, they suggested that it was far from clear that anyone really needed the incentive of a patent to invent. Opposing groups and committees of patent lawyers, engineers and large companies, who stood to gain from continued and expanded patent legislation, mobilized their political forces to support patent rights of inventors.

Unlike today, free trade advocates regarded IPRs as a privilege that could *not* be supported between jurisdictions as it constrained the free trade in goods that included claims of intellectual property. This was perhaps the last time that free traders would undertake a concerted effort to suggest that IPRs were illegitimate and fundamentally inconsistent with free trade. However, while the abolitionists had certainly stimulated a forthright debate, their dependence on largely pragmatic arguments opened the way for reform rather than the elimination of patents altogether. In the end, supporters mobilizing similar narratives of justification to those relied on today, most obviously the Lockean argument for individual reward, won the argument. As both sides shared a concern for how patents had been organized in various national jurisdictions, and between them when goods were traded internationally, these disputes were always likely to prompt reform of the system of protection, rather than its abolition.

A further element that encouraged the move to internationalize the regulation of intellectual property was, significantly, the widespread concern with "theft" by foreigners. Through extensive propaganda supporting the rights of the patent holder against the infringer and, perhaps more importantly, because of the decline of support for free trade itself, the champions of patent protection were able to preserve, and even extend, the system of intellectual property.[3] The abolitionists had supported an international agreement because, as Moureen Coulter points out, "the idea of an international agreement was the only thing that made continued domestic protection tolerable."[4] Intellectual property was still regarded as a restriction of trade, but such restrictions, as long as they served the national interest, and were applicable to all, were regarded as less problematic.

In the coming century, this frank recognition of potential conflicts between freeing international trade and intellectual property would disappear from mainstream discourse. The idea of property in knowledge became widely accepted among the governments, policy makers, and commercial interests of the increasingly developed industrialized countries, partly for pragmatic reasons and partly due to the intense lobbying of the 1860s and 1870s. This paved the way for the international market in products that stemmed from the manipulation and control of knowledge, to become formally organized on the basis of multilateral legal structures.

In 1873 the Austro-Hungarian Empire hosted a World Exposition in Vienna, but American inventors refused to take part out of concern that their inventions would not be adequately protected, and German inventors shared this reluctance. As a result of German and Austrian patent attorneys' and engineers' intense lobbying, the Austro-Hungarian government held a Congress in Vienna in the same year to address inventors' concerns.[5] The Congress endorsed international patent protection, but retained support for compulsory licensing as an instrument of public policy. The overriding objective was to establish a system in which states would recognize and protect the rights of foreign inventors and artists within states' own jurisdiction.[6] Conferences in Paris (1878 and 1880) developed the idea further and a final conference in 1883 approved and signed the Paris Convention, which was completed by an Interpretative Protocol in Madrid in 1891. The 1883 Paris Convention for the Protection of Industrial Property covered patents, trademarks, and industrial designs. Member countries also constituted an International Union for the Protection of Industrial Property, and it is in this organization that the WIPO finds its origins.

In copyright, during the nineteenth century fierce competition between French, Belgian and Swiss publishers, as well as a dense network of bilateral treaties throughout Europe, had inspired a quest for a broader multilateral agreement that would incorporate the doctrine of national treatment, where domestic and foreign authors would be treated similarly. Governments had became disenchanted with reciprocal treaties because their effects were never equal, and indeed a number of countries had refused to make such deals with France in the first half of the nineteenth century, believing that France would get the better end of any bargain. However, in 1852 Napoleon III promulgated a decree that made the counterfeiting of foreign works in France a crime punishable by law, effectively extending copyright protection to works from foreign countries whether those countries' legislation protected French works *or not*.[7] Within ten years of this French initiative, 23 additional countries signed copyright treaties with France, demonstrating a general willingness to establish the international governance of copyright provided that the benefits were shared relatively equitably.

In 1858 the French author Victor Hugo convened a Congress of Authors and Artists in Brussels that affirmed the principle of national treatment for creative artists and authors. At a subsequent conference in Paris, that ran alongside the Paris Universal Exhibition of 1878, Hugo launched the International Literary Association (later the International Literary and Artistic Association) under his founding presidency, which held a number of meetings (London 1879; Lisbon 1880; Vienna 1881; Rome 1882) culminating in the 1883 Congress in Berne. Chaired by Numa Droz, this and subsequent conventions explicitly set out to follow the example of the Paris Convention, and to produce a multilateral copyright agreement.[8] This process finally produced the Berne Convention for the Protection of Literary and

Artistic Works (1886). However, the US was excluded from this convention because it retained a provision in its copyright laws requiring authors to register their work in Washington and to send a copy to the Library of Congress. These terms were inconsistent with a convention that had made the acquisition of copyright automatic upon authorized publication in any member state. Berne signatories could not require registration as a precondition for granting copyright.

The underlying principles of both these initial multilateral intellectual property agreements were non-discrimination, national treatment and the right of priority, offering protection to the first to invent or create, rather than the first to file or reproduce. Under this system, states were free to pass legislation of their own design, but were obligated to extend their legislative protection to foreigners of member states. These conventions neither created new substantive international law nor imposed new laws on member states; rather, they reflected a consensus among member states that was legitimated by domestic laws already in place.[9] This consensus was slower to form on the other side of the Atlantic however.

The copyright battles of the nineteenth century had increasingly pitted two American factions against each other, requiring some compromise between competition and security, with battle lines drawn between competition and control. The American Copyright League formed in 1884 and, representing the elite American publishing houses such as Putnam, Houghton, Scribner, and Harper, lobbied hard for copyright reform. Even though prominent American authors such as Harriet Beecher Stowe and Mark Twain had already argued for the US to offer copyright protection for foreign works, it was only the additional pressure that the publishers brought to bear that resulted in policy change. Moral arguments notwithstanding, they and not their penny press competitors, could afford to pay for licenses to reproduce increasingly well-known foreign works.

The exclusion of America from Berne prompted the League to push for changes in US law to conform to the Berne Convention, although southern Democrats bitterly opposed any effort to open American markets to foreign competition. To appease the printing workers' unions, the final compromise of 1891, codified in the Chace Act, provided that foreign authors could obtain copyright protection only if their work was published in the United States not later than it was published in its country of origin, and foreigners' works had to be printed in the United States, or printed from type set in the United States.[10] This so-called "manufacturing clause" went directly against the Berne Convention, and therefore the US remained outside the agreement until 1986 when the clause was allowed to expire. However, in 1891 Congress signed an international agreement with England for reciprocal copyright protection.[11] Therefore, the use of such bilateral agreements that the Paris and Berne conventions had sought to end continued by virtue of US domestic policy.

An Institution is Born

Despite the major transatlantic rift over copyright in this initial period of international governance of intellectual property, the members of the Rome and Berne conventions quickly realized that there were significant commonalties between the governance of both treaties and thus it would be sensible to develop a joint secretariat. The establishment of this new secretariat in 1893 brought together the international governance of patent, copyrights and trademarks under the authority of one institution. Initially the secretariat was placed under supervision of the Swiss government with offices in Berne, where it stayed until moving to WIPO's current home in Geneva in 1960. Only when the Stockholm Conference in 1967 set out an independent international governmental organization which was established as the WIPO three years later, did it formally cease to be the responsibility of the Swiss.[12] Nevertheless, the institutionalization of the conventions' governance at the end of the nineteenth century represents the beginning of the international period of protection of intellectual property.[13] As the number of states expanded in the twentieth century so the number of members of both conventions increased and likewise the importance of the secretariat that oversaw the agreement also grew.

With the establishment of the joint secretariat for the conventions as the *Bureaux Internationaux réunis pour la protection de la propriété intellectuelle* (BIRPI), the governance of intellectual property joined a number of other commercially important sectors that jointly heralded the early origins of global governance more generally. Although communications had been the first commercial sector to establish international governance mechanisms, with the International Telegraphic Union in 1865, and the Universal Postal Union in 1874, standard-setting had followed relatively quickly with the International Bureau of Weights and Measures in 1875. Thus, the BIRPI was at the forefront of the nascent governance mechanisms that laid the foundation for late-twentieth century developments in global governance.[14] While many other elements of the post-1945 United Nations system were only established in the second half of the twentieth century, the global governance of intellectual property finds its origins much earlier.

Box 2.1: Timeline – from Berne and Paris to the establishment of the WIPO (including key treaty dates)

1850–75 – Controversy over international recognition of patents and copyrights

1858 – Brussels Congress of Authors and Artists

1873 – Vienna Congress – endorsement of international recognition of patents

1878–83 – Paris conferences to develop international patent convention

1878 – International Literary Association launched

1883 – Paris Convention for the Protection of Industrial Property

1883 – Berne Congress of International Literary Association – endorsement of international recognition of copyright

1886 – Berne Convention for the Protection of Literary and Artistic Works

1891 – Final interpretative protocol to Paris Convention adopted

1891 – Madrid Agreement for the Repression of False or Deceptive Indications of Sources on Goods

1891 – Madrid Agreement Concerning the International Recognition of Marks

1893 – Joint secretariat (for Paris and Berne conventions), Bureaux Internationaux réunis pour la protection de la propriété intellectuelle established in Berne

1908 – Failure to establish overarching international protection for music-related copyrights at Berlin Convention – national flexibility retained

1925 – Hague Agreement Concerning the International Deposit of Industrial Designs

1928 – Compromise for broadcasts at Rome Convention, similar to 1908 Berlin Convention

1952 – Universal Copyright Convention established by UNESCO

1958 – Lisbon Agreement for the Protection of Appellations of Origin and their International Registration

1961 – Rome Convention reduced national flexibilities in music and broadcast copyright

1962 – Demands for Bureaux to become formal international orga-
       nization
1963 – First non-Swiss Director appointed
1967 – Stockholm conference formalizes arrangements (including
       budgetary control)
1970 – The World Intellectual Property Organization is established
1970 – Patent Co-operation Treaty concluded
1971 – Geneva Convention for the Protection of Producers of
       Phonograms Against the Unauthorized Duplication of their
       Phonograms
1971 – Strasbourg Agreement Concerning the International
       Patent Classification
1974 – The WIPO becomes a specialized agency of the United
       Nations

During the first half of the twentieth century, the BIRPI oversaw a
number of further treaties and amendments to the original conventions.
These were often responses to new technologies in various economic
sectors where IPRs were becoming more important, but also represented
successful lobbying by a number of private sector groups that were
eager to ensure that IPRs were both protected and extended. However,
commercial interests were not always shared among sectors and at the
convention that resulted in the Berlin 1908 revisions to the Berne
Convention, for instance, whereas the book publishers were happy with
a system of exclusive rights to authorize publication which could be
purchased and exploited, the newly emergent music recordings industry
considered it more important in a fast moving field to allow competing
record companies to record the same piece of music and accompanying
lyrics. This dispute between sectors resulted in a return to national
distinctions over this issue.[15] Given that the conventions regulated
private commercial relations, states were often willing to respond to
pressure from their domestic industries' representatives, but not always.

When BIRPI members met in Rome in 1928 to deal with issues
raised by new broadcasting technologies, there were clear differences of
opinion between states that wanted to reserve the private rights for
authors as they already did for other technologies of distribution, and
those countries like Australia and New Zealand that saw broadcasting
as a public service that should be unencumbered by private rights,
reflecting the emerging public service ethos of broadcasting in

countries with vast distances between small communities. Once again, a compromise solution was concluded that, while setting the parameters of choice, allowed individual states to shape the measures that were appropriate for their societies.[16] Thus, during this period significant national variance in domestic regulation of intellectual property remained, and even when many of these broadcast issues were encompassed in the 1961 Rome Convention, the convention was unable to attract the number of signatories that the preceding more flexible conventions had.[17] Broadcasting remained an area where many states wished to retain their autonomy.

As more and more new states emerged during the post-1945 period of accelerated decolonialization, the membership profile of the BIRPI started to shift from being dominated by industrialized and developed states. Newly independent countries' governments were often keen to establish their membership of international society by joining various multilateral agreements and international organizations. The member governments of the BIRPI saw the potential for encouraging these "new" states to join and by doing so expand the realm of governance for intellectual property, which would potentially benefit the export oriented companies in their own national intellectual property-related sectors. These new members, many of which were newly emerged states, wanted the established countries to recognize their interests, reflecting the newly global democratic structures of the UN and its General Assembly. Thus, in the 1950s and into the 1960s, the conferences organized by the BIRPI began to include delegations that were sharply critical of the manner in which intellectual property was being utilized in the international system.

Already many of the issues that would become familiar in later debates about the relationship between intellectual property and development were being raised and discussed, before the WIPO itself was formally established. As Andréa Koury Menescal has argued at some length, many of the issues that were recently included in the proposal for a Development Agenda at the WIPO are remarkably similar to the draft resolution on intellectual property that was put before the UN by Brazil in 1961.[18] This included concerns about technology transfer, the abuse of patent monopolies, and the need to focus on the end of development, alongside an explicit denial that such an agenda was a demand for the abolition of the current system. However, after considerable debate and maneuvering, the resulting UN resolution 16/1713, adopted on 19 December 1961, firmly placed the examination and possible revision of the system with the BIRPI, rather than an independent body. The subsequent series of conferences and reports, involving the International

Chamber of Commerce and the Association for the Protection of Intellectual Property, alongside the BIRPI, effectively stifled the intent of the resolution, leaving the issues to re-emerge some 40 years later.

At this time, in the early 1960s, the BIRPI's staff were well aware that other international organizations, not least of all the UN Economic and Social Council, were exploring the possibility of developing a more formal role in the international governance of IPRs.[19] Indeed, the International Labor Organization had also been showing some interest in IPR-related issues on behalf of workers, and partly as a response to the problem of the US being outside the Berne Convention, had in 1952, in consort with the United Nations Education Scientific and Cultural Organization (UNESCO) helped establish the Universal Copyright Convention (revised in 1971). This alternative copyright convention operated as a clear alternative center of diplomatic gravity to the BIRPI, further stimulating the exploration of a more formalized institutional existence.

Until this point the *Bureaux* had enjoyed a slightly anomalous existence in the realm of multilateral agencies, being at once both international and predominantly the responsibility of the Swiss government. Therefore, at the 1962 meeting of the Permanent Bureau of the Paris Union and Berne Union, a committee of experts was set up to explore the possibility of establishing the *Bureaux* as a more normal international organization, and to that end a diplomatic conference was organized. Moreover, as a move to making the *Bureaux* more clearly *inter*national, in 1963 the Swiss government appointed, for the first time in the organization's history, a non-Swiss as Director: Georg H. C. Bodenhausen, from the Netherlands. With Bodenhausen as Director, and Arpad Bogsch as Deputy, a number of "preparations for the 'structural and administrative' reform (an expression coined for the purpose and consistently used in the official documents) were pursued with thoroughness and speed."[20] After a second meeting of the Permanent Bureau, attended by 39 member states, of which nine were developing countries, a draft convention consolidating the previous governance arrangements into a formal international organization was taken to the 1967 Stockholm Conference, where the convention was approved, thereby facilitating the establishment of the WIPO three years later.[21] One of the key changes accomplished by the conference, and preparatory to the shift in status, was the assumption of responsibility for the budget, program and activities of the organization by its members, removing this responsibility from the Swiss government which up until this time had effectively controlled the organization. This change of arrangements facilitated the successful application by the WIPO to become a specialized agency of the United Nations in 1974.

The World Intellectual Property Organization and the United Nations

The move to become a specialized agency of the UN was primarily driven by Arpad Bogsch, first as Deputy Director of the BIRPI from 1963, then as Deputy Director General of the WIPO on its formation, and finally as Director General from 1973 to his retirement in 1997. Bogsch strove to establish the WIPO as a universal organization for the protection of intellectual property and saw the link with the UN as a crucial mechanism to this end. Unsurprisingly, his first major move as the new Director General was to initiate proceedings to gain specialized agency status. Indeed, the organizational structure of the WIPO was established so that it already resembled that of a UN specialized agency, making the assumption of this status easy to complete.[22]

Unfortunately, the strategy of universalization was at odds with the developing countries' interests in establishing a New International Economic Order, that stressed national autonomy over IPR-related policy, most obviously in the realm of compulsory licenses, and over issues relating to technology transfer.[23] Nevertheless, Borgsch's desire to link up with the UN also prompted the WIPO to agree to be listed as co-author on the 1974 United Nations Conference on Trade and Development (UNCTAD) report *The Role of the Patent System in the Transfer of Technology to Developing Countries*, despite the report's thrust being widely divergent from the WIPO's position on the role of patents in technological transfer.[24] Thus, the WIPO was shaped from the start by Borgsch's vision of universalization, but the seeds of some of the WIPO's more recent problems were also sown by his assumption that the link with the UN would further this end.

While universalization was a key motive for the assumption of specialized agency status it was not the only perceived advantage: the *Bureaux* and specifically Bogsch believed that working inside the UN system would also encourage developing countries to join the organization, and would enable the internal administration of the organization to benefit from the economies of scale available inside the UN.[25] The proposed widening of the membership prompted some concerns among the already existing member states, as their representatives (rightly as it turned out) were worried that these new developing country members might question and undermine the key *promotional* aspects of the WIPO's activities. Conversely, many of the new members were very concerned about the limitations on staff recruitment that seemed to be implied by the WIPO's establishing convention, that stressed the use of technical experts to discuss their problems. For a number of developing country delegates at the diplomatic meetings that finalized the WIPO's convention, this suggested that critics and those with non-orthodox views about the value and use of IPRs would be excluded from the organization.[26] Again these early concerns have resurfaced in the more recent debates regarding the activities of the WIPO in the new millennium.

Like all specialized agencies of the UN, the WIPO is formally an independent organization with its own members. Although to a large extent it shares the UN's membership, there is no necessary co-membership between the two organizations. For example, for many years, until Switzerland joined the UN at the end of the last century, it was an important and influential member of the WIPO, having played a major role in the establishment and maintenance of its predecessor organization, but was not a member of the UN. However, although independent organizationally, as a specialized agency of the UN, the WIPO was, and is, required to work in accordance with the UN's overall developmental mission. Indeed, the manner in which the notion of development has been conceived of at the WIPO has become an area of some tension, which we will return to in chapter five.

Unlike other parts of the UN network of organizations, the WIPO is largely funded by fees that the private sector pays for the use of the Patent Co-operation Treaty (PCT). Thus, although it is a specialized agency, the WIPO is freed from many of the budget-related pressures that shape and sometimes constrain other UN organizations. While the member countries do make a small contribution to the running costs of the organization this is minimal, with the five largest country contributors accounting for less than three percent of the annual budget between them. This has meant that the richer members have been unable to effectively control the organization through their control over the budget.

The link with the UN allowed the WIPO to gain both diplomatic advantage from being a member of the UN system, as well as demonstrating its central role in the realm of global economic governance. As a specialized agency of the UN the WIPO became party to the Convention on Privileges and Immunities of Specialized Agencies.[27] The primary advantages to the WIPO of this formalized link are the assumption of international legal personality (article II), that means it is treated as a sovereign contracting individual for the purposes of international law, and most importantly in the realm of treaty obligations, as well as the extension of the diplomatic privileges and immunities (article V and VI) enjoyed by state representatives and staff members of the UN to the state representatives and staff of the WIPO.

These diplomatic advantages include the "laissez-passer" (free passage) unrestricted travel of the organization's representatives and staff, which was also explicitly included as article 17 of the formal agreement between the UN and the WIPO.

Those working at the WIPO therefore become members of the international diplomatic community, and as such this has become a significant element in the organization's program to recruit to its staff positions a group of like-minded experts that shared the WIPO's goals and interests.[28] Additionally, by extending the status and advantages of international diplomacy to various experts, the WIPO was able to build a community that it could then draw on for "independent" expert advice for its members, but advice that was shaped by the WIPO's own agenda. The UN link gave the WIPO a mechanism for maintaining and expanding a group of supportive academics and lawyers who enjoyed significant travel and diplomatic privileges in service of the WIPO's various developmental and assistance programs, and who had something to lose if they significantly diverged from the WIPO's expressed position on any issue.

The formal agreement with the UN set out how the two organizations would co-ordinate their activities and co-operate over their strategic direction, with an obligation by the WIPO to follow any recommendations of the UN and work with other agencies to develop resources to tackle problems identified by the WIPO and the other specialized agencies (article 5).[29] Alongside various commitments related to information and documents (article 6), the provision of statistics (article 7) and technical assistance (article 9), the WIPO also undertook through this agreement to facilitate the transfer of technology. Explicitly, the WIPO was obliged to work with the UNCTAD, the UNDP (United Nations Development Program) and the UNIDO (United Nations Industrial Development Organization) to promote and facilitate "the transfer of technology to developing countries in such a manner as to assist these countries in attaining *their* objectives in the fields of science and technology and trade and development" (article 10, emphasis added). This question of how the WIPO's activities have interacted with, and have often differed from, developing countries' priorities has become a major element in the criticisms leveled at the WIPO.

Nevertheless, since 1974, the link with the UN has focussed the WIPO's attention not merely on administrating the treaties it oversees, and more specifically running the PCT, but also has required the organization to work with developing countries to develop their domestic legislation as regards intellectual property, not least of all through the Co-operation for Development Program (see chapter three). This was made clear in the first report that the WIPO submitted to the UN in 1975, reporting on its activities in its first year as a specialized agency. The statement stressed that:

> As in the case of all organizations of the United Nations system, one of the main objectives of [the] WIPO is to assist developing countries in their development. [The] WIPO assists developing countries in promoting their industrialization, their commerce and their cultural, scientific and technological development through the modernization of their industrial property and copyright systems and in meeting some of their needs in scientific documentation and the transfer of technology and technical know-how.[30]

As is still the case to this day, the assistance offered ranged from training of administrators to the provision of model laws, including seminars and other meetings to discuss key intellectual property issues, and help drafting members' legislation. However, perhaps most interestingly given subsequent criticisms of its activities, the WIPO statement also explicitly reported that the organization aimed to facilitate the transfer of technology under "fair and reasonable terms and conditions."[31] In the last few years, this reassurance has been subject to sustained criticism both from the WIPO's own developing country members and various non-governmental organizations.

Although the WIPO has continued to function as a specialized agency of the UN and plays a continuing role in the global governance of IPRs, the establishment of the World Trade Organization (WTO) with a new overarching agreement on intellectual property as one of its key elements was a major challenge to the WIPO and its methods of governance. Before examining this challenge, the next section briefly explores the background to the TRIPs agreement, not least as it is the context in which the most recent political economy of the WIPO has been played out.

The Negotiation of the TRIPs Agreement

By the time of the launch of the Uruguay Round of multilateral trade negotiations in 1986, developed countries' governments and their negotiators had started to see that the issue of IPRs, their protection and use, was likely to become increasingly important in future international trade relations. The expanding possibilities for technical appropriation of knowledge or information, alongside widespread counterfeit reproduction and distribution of knowledge-based products, prompted the rich and industrialized countries' governments to act on behalf of their national corporate interests. Indeed, a major element in the political pressure to include the protection and enforcement of IPRs in the Uruguay Round originated in the response by the content industries to a series of information technology-related innovations. These both enhanced the possibilities of an international (commodity) trade in information- and knowledge-related goods, *and* enlarged the perceived possibilities of "theft" and "piracy."

A group of US corporations formed the Intellectual Property Committee (IPC) that not only aimed to bring pressure to bear on the American government to get IPRs on to the agenda for negotiation, but also provided considerable legal support to the negotiating team.[32] Crucially, the IPC's influence was not limited to US trade negotiators: it also worked hard to convince industrial associations in Europe and Japan that a new governance regime for IPRs was possible, and then mobilized them to support its quest to include intellectual property protection in the Uruguay Round. These three groups then worked together to produce a consensual document, rooted in industrialized countries' laws, on fundamental principles for a multilateral approach to intellectual property protection. This document was then presented to the GATT secretariat and Geneva-based representatives of numerous countries.

This process, in which industry played such a central role, was unprecedented for the GATT, although the private sector had for many decades played a major role in the negotiations at the BIRPI and then the WIPO. While the IPC derived its influence from the economic resources and power it represented in the US domestic economy, its characterization of itself as representing the crucial sectors of the new information-based economy helped it establish the negotiating framework for the TRIPs agreement. This was undoubtedly aided by the increasingly shrill proclamations of the imminent "new age" from think-tanks and in the media.[33] Supported by the US, the IPC was able to broadly get the agreement on intellectual property it wanted. The US government had begun to see these information-related industries as the competitive and crucial sectors for maintaining US economic strength, and the Office of the United States Trade Representative (USTR) took the IPC's demands very seriously. Furthermore, given the general perception of the specialized nature of intellectual property law, the IPC capitalized on the assumption that extensive technical knowledge was needed to "support" the negotiating teams. Thus, the IPC essentially drafted the TRIPs agreement while the actual negotiations fine-tuned the text and made some concessions to developing countries' negotiators.

Trade negotiators themselves had already concluded that the complex of 24 multilateral treaties previously administered by the WIPO produced too much rule diversity. Even within each agreement there was considerable variance in the scope of protection offered. For instance, in 1988 a study for the WIPO's TRIPs negotiating group had discovered that of the 98 signatories to the Paris Convention, over 40 excluded from their legislation pharmaceutical products, animal varieties, methods of treatment, plant varieties, and biological processes for producing animal and plant varieties, while over 30 excluded food products and computer programs, and a further 22 excluded chemical products.[34] Making the problem more complex, it was not necessarily the same group of country-members excluding specific sets of categories. Led by the USTR, developed countries' negotiators suggested, for the purposes of clarity in the international trade of IPR-related products, that there was a clear benefit to be gained from a unified agreement. This line of argument did little to stimulate developing countries' governments' interest in including IPRs in multilateral trade negotiations.

Therefore, to encourage a change of heart regarding the negotiation of the TRIPs agreement, the USTR threatened bilateral trade sanctions (under the Special 301 section of the Omnibus Trade and Tariff Act, 1988), and actually utilized these measures against a range of targets, including a majority of those developing countries whose governments had been active in opposing the position of the US in the TRIPs negotiating group.[35] This stick was combined with the carrot of a promise to open up agricultural markets and an offer to abolish the Multi-Fiber Arrangement which constrained developing countries' textile exports.[36] The USTR also negotiated a number of bilateral trade and investment treaties with developing countries that included provisions that moved these countries towards a TRIPs-model of IPR protection. This lessened resistance to TRIPs compliance as after concluding these agreements and making the required legal changes, there was less legislative distance between domestic provisions and TRIPs-compliant legislation.[37] Many developing countries lacked the expertise and resources to fully resist this firm bilateral pressure.

The divide and rule strategy of selectively withdrawing General System of Preference (GSP) market access provisions also worked against the maintenance of a collective developing countries' negotiating bloc.[38] Although even in 1989 it was clear to many commentators and negotiators what the likely detrimental effects of an international trade agreement on IPRs would be, this was not the same as being able to withstand the considerable political resources that the developed countries' negotiators brought to bear to secure the TRIPs agreement. The combination of political pressure, and weakened resistance due to the complexity of the negotiations, relative to the limited resources developing countries' governments could dedicate to them, ensured that when the developing countries joined the new WTO they had to accede, with some transitional arrangements, to the TRIPs agreement as well.[39]

Ironically the original pressure to amend the international system governing intellectual property had not originated in the US or other developed countries, but with the Group of 77 some years before. During the 1960s and 1970s, developing countries' governments were worried about the problems of economic development and seized upon patent protection as one of the factors behind import monopolies and the failure to develop indigenous technologies.[40] As noted above this had prompted Brazil's proposal to reform the international patent system in 1961. At that time, the institutions of intellectual property were perceived not as organs of free trade, as they would be characterized in the TRIPs agreement, but as tools of protection for the owners of IPRs in the rich and developed countries. Such arguments had striking similarities with positions adopted in the debates that had preceded the Paris and Berne conventions in the nineteenth century. The utilization of IPRs maintained the technology gap and uneven development or underdevelopment. This led developing countries' governments to be antagonistic towards demands that their national legislation should accord similar levels of protection to IPRs that were enjoyed in the US, Europe or Japan. Thus, during the 1960s and 1970s the developing countries' governments argued for a *dilution* of international intellectual property law, while the developed countries' governments merely supported the status quo.

The key distinction between the position of the Group of 77 and the developed countries rested on the purpose of protecting patents and other IPRs. For the developing countries' governments the most important factor was their own countries' development and the narrowing of the technology gap. The rich countries' negotiating position, which in the end was consolidated by the TRIPs agreement, was that the rights belonging to owners, and therefore the sanctity of their property, was paramount. Only by ensuring the property rights of innovators and entrepreneurs were protected from theft could any national economy hope to develop and support economic growth. However, the developing countries' governments often used their national legislation to reduce the monopoly rights accorded to intellectual property, enjoying the flexibility that the WIPO-governed system extended to states.

Developing countries had received some support in this policy from the UNCTAD, most explicitly in the 1975 report *The International Patent System as an Instrument for National Development*, which was exclusively devoted to the question of revising the Paris Convention, sharply criticizing existing arrangements and urging reforms to improve the situation of developing countries.[41] Some diplomats suspected that developing countries' governments were using patents as a scapegoat for more difficult problems internal to their economies. Nevertheless, in 1980 the Diplomatic Conference for the Revision of the Paris Convention was convened, but the series of four conferences organized by the WIPO remained deadlocked by the opposed views of the purpose of IPR protection, leaving the developing countries' negotiators' attempt to widen the public realm for intellectual property frustrated.

Having opened the debates about intellectual property revision, the developing countries' governments subsequently found themselves overtaken by events. While many developing countries' governments still considered it a development issue, for the developed countries' negotiators in the 1980s, knowledge-based industries' intellectual properties were now an invaluable and crucial resource linked to competitiveness and trade. This had already begun to radically shift domestic legislation, utilizing the flexibilities in the WIPO to strengthen protection, and it was not long before a similar dynamic was informing international policy as well. The differences between the supporters of IPRs and those more critical of their worth were clearly articulated during the negotiations that led to the TRIPs agreement, although those developing countries that were party to the negotiations were ultimately unsuccessful in shifting the content of the agreement to any great degree. Indeed, some developing countries' negotiators also perceived advantages to an agreement.

Certainly, the cross-issue linkage suggested that agreement on IPRs could be used to leverage other trade benefits, of which markets access in textiles and agriculture were the most important. Many negotiators, seeing the prospect of a growing bilateralism in IPRs, also regarded a multilateral agreement such as TRIPs as a better alternative. Furthermore, by the last decade of the twentieth century some of the richer developing countries' governments were being lobbied by domestic businesses seeking some form of IPR-related protection in specific sectors.[42] Thus, while the negotiations may have been lopsided, many developing countries' governments could still see that there were some national advantages to be gained.

Although at the beginning the debate might have been character-ized as a North–South difference over the fundamentals of protecting IPRs, as the negotiations gathered pace, the majority of meeting time was spent on trying to resolve the differences between the positions of the US, Europe and Japan over the protection of IPRs, leaving the concerns of the developing countries marginalized.[43] In 1990 the developing countries' negotiators were still expressing concern that the negotia-tions continued to treat IPRs exclusively as a commercial matter and that insufficient account was being taken of national development priorities. However, by this point the battle had been lost, and the possibility of retaining the WIPO's system of variable commitments and flexibilities essentially disappeared.

The TRIPs agreement was the result of a political process, driven by specific industrial and national interests, not merely the consolidation of a set of legitimated regulatory provisions, with differences only regarding their implementation. The TRIPS agreement incorporates a notion of IPRs as a system of exclusion and protection rather than one of diffu-sion and competition. It extends rightsholders' privileges and reduces their obligations. This far-reaching agreement has important implications for innovation, research and development, economic development, the future location of industry, and the global division of labor. Indeed, the dramatic expansion of the scope of IPRs embodied in the agreement reduces the options available to future industrializers by blocking the route that their predecessors followed. It raises the price of information and technology by extending the monopoly privileges of rightsholders, and requires states to play a much greater role in defending them.

TRIPs' Challenge to the World Intellectual Property Organization

One of the key reasons that the developed countries, led by the US and EU negotiators, wanted to move the global governance of IPRs into the remit of the new WTO, was the desire to strengthen the mecha-nisms of international enforcement of IPRs. This clearly reflected badly on the WIPO, or at least demonstrated the lack of commitment to the organization by those countries whose corporations controlled significant intellectual property-related resources. In the next chapter we will examine how the WIPO has reorganized its working patterns now that the global governance of IPRs is underpinned by the TRIPs agreement. However, the establishment of the TRIPs agreement itself represented a significant challenge to the WIPO, perhaps most obviously as it removed sole responsibility for the international governance of intellectual property from the WIPO and firmly placed it with the WTO, while allowing some continuity of function for the WIPO.

This challenge to the WIPO's competence reflects what is often termed "forum shopping" in international diplomatic negotiations. Negotiators from the US and the EU understood clearly that firstly they were unable to secure agreements on the extension to, and toughening up of, the global regulation of IPRs at the WIPO because of its internal organization. Secondly, and perhaps more importantly, prompted by the demands of major domestic industrial groups, these negotiators saw considerable promise for the consolidation and expansion of regulation through the link with the wider realm of international trade. It was not the first time that such forum shifting had been deployed in the realm of intellectual property; when the US had continued to be unable for domestic reasons to join the Berne Convention, it acceded to the Universal Copyright Convention (through UNESCO) as an alternative regulatory mechanism for its international trade in copyrighted products.[44] Thus, given the difficulties that the WIPO had experienced in the realm of enforcement, it is perhaps no surprise that trade diplomats from the developed countries should become exasperated and seek an alternative governance mechanism better suited to their needs.

As Laurence Helfer has noted, there were three institutional advantages offered by the expanded and globalized regime of trade governance that made the WTO more suitable to the major developed countries interested in the strengthening of governance for intellectual property. Firstly, the trade negotiations had always been conducted on the basis of consensus rather than unanimity, and thus there could be significant advances on the basis of the developed countries' agenda, even if there were significant objections, as these could be sidelined through the manipulation of the complex negotiations of which IPRs would only be one part. Secondly, and reflecting the leverage of market access to developing countries' economies, not only did the US and EU have significant leverage in trade negotiations, by being able to link sectors and markets together in omnibus agreements, they could buy off objections on the basis of offering concessions over tariffs and obstructions in other markets of more immediate interest to developing countries. Finally, although it was the case that dispute settlement at the GATT was already a lot more effective than any enforcement at the WIPO, the establishment in 1995 of the robust dispute settlement mechanism at the new WTO gave the developed countries a weapon for enforcing the regulation they wanted, that they had never had before.[45] Thus many aspects of the WIPO that were valued by its developing country members underpinned the reasons for the US and EU seeking a new forum.

The negotiation of the TRIPs agreement again demonstrated the difficulties that the WIPO had suffered as regards its most important members; those that controlled most intellectual property. The settlement that emerged in the wake of the establishment of the WTO divided the global governance of intellectual property into two distinct realms.[46] On one side the political disputes were to be conducted at the WTO and through its specialized TRIPs Council. Here, debates about the extension of regulations and questions about the modification of the TRIPs agreement itself are subject to ongoing (and often fraught) negotiation. On the other side, the WTO recognized the value of employing the WIPO's extensive resources to support training and development in the developing countries. Moreover, as we will see later, the move to the WTO as a negotiating forum was hardly comprehensive. Thus, we might better refer to the shift as *forum proliferation* rather than a uni-directional forum shift.

The relationship between the WIPO and the WTO has taken the form not merely of a de facto division of labor, but has involved an agreement on how the two organizations will work together to manage the TRIPs agreement and the governance of IPRs more widely, formalized in the WTO–WIPO cooperation agreement of 1 January 1996.[47] While such an arrangement might have been hoped to have some pragmatic advantages, not least of all that the WIPO might have hoped to restrict its exposure to political criticism, the period since the establishment of the TRIPs agreement has seen the politics of intellectual property become more and more central to global politics. Perhaps realizing that the organization could not hide behind a claim merely to be a technical organization for ever, in 1998 Kamil Idris, the incoming Director General, set up the Global Intellectual Property Issues Division (GIPID) to identify new technological and political issues or problems that might arise from new patterns of globalization.[48] However, while the original remit of the division was relatively wide, in subsequent years it has increasingly focussed on issues around the exploitation and protection of traditional knowledge and three years after its establishment was renamed the Traditional Knowledge Division.

Like the WIPO's activities in other areas, the Traditional Knowledge Division can be seen as part of a program to promote intellectual property to groups either unaware of, or hostile to, the use of property rights in the realm of information and knowledge. In this sense, as the following chapters will reveal, at the heart of most debates and analyses of the WIPO's activities, is this question of the *promotion* of intellectual property. Even when divisions were explicitly set up to avoid the explicit establishment of norms (as was the GIPID and its successor Traditional Knowledge Division), the normalizing of an approach that puts intellectual property into the agenda of discussion relating to this and other issues, such as bio-genetic resources, is itself, by implication, laying the groundwork for normative change. Thus, despite the clear shift of its competencies and authority in the post-TRIPs period, it would be wrong to assume that the WIPO has been effectively marginalized or is no longer of any importance. Rather, what we have seen is a shift in the manner in which the WIPO works within the structures of global governance: it has become a much more focussed agency, leaving enforcement to the WTO and now concentrating on socialization and norm-building.

3 How the WIPO works

Having laid out the historical context of the World Intellectual Property Organization, we will now turn to the shape of the organization and how it functions in Geneva. Despite the increasingly global realm of the so-called knowledge economy, the WIPO remains an inter-governmental organization because intellectual property is still regulated and governed by domestic law. Although these laws need to comply with World Trade Organization (WTO) members' commitments under the Trade Related Aspects of Intellectual Property Rights (TRIPs) agreement, the actual legislation producing the required protections and rights remains the subject of national political deliberation. Nevertheless, many states adopt legislation in line with model laws provided by the WIPO and/or the "best practice" of developed countries. As noted in the previous chapter, after the establishment of the WTO with the TRIPs agreement as one of its key elements, the WIPO's direct governance activities were circumscribed. The WIPO no longer has any enforcement duties as regards the various treaties it once oversaw; since 1995 these have been largely incorporated into the TRIPs agreement. However, the WIPO continues to have a significant administrative and support function, as well as again becoming the chosen forum for negotiating further extensions to the global governance regime for intellectual property.

After the changes prompted by the conclusion of the Uruguay Round of multilateral trade negotiations, the WIPO's three principal areas of operation are: registration; technical support; and development of further governance measures.[1] The first of these activities is primarily concerned with the administration of the Patent Cooperation Treaty (PCT); this involves the processing of applications under the PCT and as such is a direct service to owners of, and applicants for, patents in various jurisdictions. Alongside this PCT-related activity the WIPO also processes the international registration of trademarks (under the Madrid System), acts as a depository for internationally deployed industrial designs (under the Hague Agreement) and acts as a registry for applications for appellations of origin (under the Lisbon Agreement). These activities provide the majority of the funds for the rest of the WIPO's undertakings.

This income has allowed the WIPO to maintain some partial independence; unlike other specialized agencies of the United Nations, it is not dependent on the UN for any significant part of its annual budget. Although the WIPO is still subject to political influence, and the demands of its richer and most powerful members, superficially it has more independence than most other major international organizations in the contemporary constellation of global governance. However, it is worth stressing that I am not suggesting that the WIPO is therefore an independent, non-aligned organization; rather, although it is at least partly independent of major state politics, nevertheless by virtue of its *promotional* mode of activity as regards intellectual property rights (IPRs), it frequently underpins and supports the position of the most developed states in the global system. Here, the formal appearance of independence can sometimes add weight to its political position, an issue to which we will return.

The second area of activities concerns technical support and assistance to help members build the capacity to manage the protection and regulation of IPRs to fulfill their international obligations due to membership of the WTO or where particular members of the WIPO have agreed bilateral trade or investment treaties that involve undertakings regarding the protection of intellectual property. This support ranges from information dissemination activities, including collections of members' existing laws for guidance to policy makers developing new legislation, to a wide-ranging education and training program. Indeed, since 1993 the WIPO's own Academy in Geneva has offered a diverse range of residential courses and more recently has developed an extensive on-line learning program. This is intended to "enable the participants after returning to their respective countries, to become active in the formulation of government policies on intellectual property questions."[2]

The third area of the WIPO's activities involves the promotion of compliance with existing treaties, including those now encompassed by the TRIPs agreement, as well as the updating and revision of these treaties in response to members' requirements, and the organization of negotiations towards the development of new treaties in the realm of intellectual property. Most obviously this aspect of the organization's current activities has been taken up with its multifaceted response to the increasingly global reach of digitized communication.

To govern these activities the WIPO has a General Assembly, which consists of all states that are members of the WIPO, and that are also members of one or more of the treaties that the WIPO formally oversees. The General Assembly appoints the Director General, who is nominated by the Coordination Committee, the executive branch of the WIPO, and oversees the activities of the executive and the Director General, reviewing and approving their actions. The General Assembly also has control of the budget, and determines which non-members (including states, other intergovernmental organizations and international non-governmental organizations) should have observer status at the WIPO. Observer status (as of mid-2005) was enjoyed by 66 IGOs (including all the main UN agencies, the main regional intellectual property organizations, a number of sectoral or issue-focussed organizations, alongside 29 regional IGOs), 180 INGOs and 13 national NGOs.[3]

The Conference of the WIPO consists of all states that are members of the WIPO even if they are signatories to none of its treaties. The Conference can make recommendations based on the deliberation of the members on any aspect of the WIPO's activities. It shapes the development cooperation program, thereby directing the organization's technical support, and adopts a budget for this purpose. The

Box 3.1

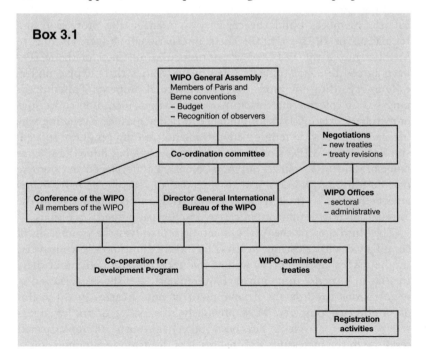

Conference can also adopt amendments to the WIPO's establishing convention proposed by the state members, the Coordination Committee or the Director General, and like the Assembly can authorize non-state actors to become official observers.

The Coordination Committee and the office of the Director General (the International Bureau of the WIPO) serve the two general organs of the organization. The Coordination Committee advises both the General Assembly and the Conference on the budget and issues related to the various treaties. The Committee also prepares the draft agenda of the General Assembly and of the Conference, as well as the draft program and budget for the Conference's activities. The International Bureau of the WIPO is headed by the Director General and acts as the secretariat of the organization. The Bureau runs the operations of the WIPO on a day-to-day basis in light of the programs adopted and approved by the General Assembly and the Conference. However, as with most international organizations, while formally serving the membership, due to its permanent character, and the expertise of its staff, the work of the International Bureau and the interests of its staff have a significant influence on the strategy, practices and focus of the WIPO. Like all specialized agencies of the UN, the International Bureau staff are recruited in accordance with the UN's principle of equitable geographical distribution.

There are three types of treaties that the WIPO is concerned with.[4] The first, treaties that establish international protection, have now been largely incorporated within the remit of the WTO. Although the WIPO still maintains some oversight of these major treaties covering patents, copyrights, trademarks and geographical indicators, they are largely now managed within the global trade governance regime. However, the WIPO remains involved with the treaties that facilitate the international recognition of specific intellectual properties; as noted above, these international registration activities are one of the three main areas of activity for the WIPO. Finally, the WIPO is responsible for improving and updating a number of treaties that establish classification systems for intellectual property.

Although those treaties for the regulation and enforcement of IPRs that were incorporated into the TRIPs agreement now have a similar geographic range as the WTO, those treaties that are still overseen by the WIPO remain unevenly and differentially ratified. This is the problem that prompted the move to international trade-related governance by the developed countries during the Uruguay Round in the 1980s and early 1990s. This non-symmetrical membership was previously seen by US and EU negotiators as a serious enforcement

Box 3.2: Treaties administrated by the World Intellectual Property Organization, with number of WIPO signatories (mid-2005)

- WIPO Convention: Convention Establishing the World Intellectual Property Organization (1967; amended in 1979)
- Paris Convention for the Protection of Industrial Property (1883; revised at Brussels (1900), Washington (1911), The Hague (1925), London (1934), Lisbon (1958) and Stockholm (1967), and amended in 1979)
  [169 signatories]
- Berne Convention for the Protection of Literary and Artistic Work (1886; completed at Paris (1896), revised at Berlin (1908), completed at Berne (1914), revised at Rome (1928), at Brussels (1948), at Stockholm (1967) and at Paris (1971), and amended in 1979)
  [159 signatories]
- Madrid Agreement for the Repression of False or Deceptive Indications of Source on Goods (1891; revised at Washington (1911), The Hague (1925), London (1934) and Lisbon (1958), and supplemented by the Additional Act of Stockholm (1967))
  [34 signatories]
- Madrid Agreement Concerning the International Registration of Marks (1891; revised at Brussels (1900), Washington (1911), The Hague (1925), London (1934), Nice (1957) and Stockholm (1967), and amended in 1979)
  [56 signatories]
- Hague Agreement Concerning the International Deposit of Industrial Designs (1925; revised at London (1934) and The Hague (1960), supplemented by the Additional Act of Monaco (1961), the Complementary Act of Stockholm (1967) and the Protocol of Geneva (1975), and amended in 1979)
  [42 signatories]
- Nice Agreement Concerning the International Classification of Goods and Services for the Purposes of the Registration of Marks (1957; revised at Stockholm (1967) and at Geneva (1977), and amended in 1979)
  [75 signatories]

- Lisbon Agreement for the Protection of Appellations of Origin and Their International Registration (1958; revised at Stockholm (1967), and amended in 1979)
  [23 signatories]
- Rome Convention: International Convention for the Protection of Performers, Producers of Phonograms and Broadcasting Organizations (1961)
  [79 signatories]
- Locarno Agreement Establishing an International Classification for Industrial Designs (1968; amended in 1979)
  [45 signatories]
- PCT: Patent Cooperation Treaty (Washington (1970), amended in 1979 and modified in 1984)
  [126 signatories]
- Strasbourg Agreement Concerning the International Patent Classification (1971, amended in 1979)
  [55 signatories]
- Phonograms Convention: Convention for the Protection of Producers of Phonograms Against Unauthorized Duplication of Their Phonograms (Geneva, 1971)
  [74 signatories]
- Vienna Agreement Establishing an International Classification of the Figurative Elements of Marks (1973, amended in 1985)
  [20 signatories]
- Budapest Treaty on the International Recognition of the Deposit of Microorganisms for the Purposes of Patent Procedure (1977, modified in 1980)
  [60 signatories]
- Nairobi Treaty on the Protection of the Olympic Symbol (1981)
  [43 signatories]
- Trademark Law Treaty (Geneva, 1994)
  [33 signatories]

problem. However, now that these negotiators are seeking to move beyond the "floor" that the TRIPs agreement has established, the ability to mediate agreements on further treaties between smaller groups of members of the WIPO has become a positive advantage as regards the incremental raising of standards of protection. Thus, while in the past the WIPO had been criticized for facilitating a complex and divergent group of agreements reflecting variances in national interests, this is now useful to those countries' governments pushing for further expansion of protection of IPRs, given the increasingly trenchant resistance by many developing countries to such moves. However before examining the political disputes that have begun to engulf the global governance of IPRs, we need to understand the WIPO's place in the governance structure in more detail.

Patent Cooperation Treaty and Other Registration Activities

Of all the treaties that the WIPO oversees, for budgetary reasons, the PCT is perhaps the most important. The WIPO's stewardship of this agreement allows it effective budgetary independence, to some extent immunizing the organization from political pressure, in contrast to other agencies of the UN. The PCT itself was the WIPO's response to the growing disquiet during the 1960s among multinational corporations, especially those based in the US, regarding the costs and organizational effort of making multiple patent applications across the jurisdictions in which they operated. The PCT was mapped out in its essentials late in the 1960s by the then US Commissioner of Patents, Edward J. Brenner, and Arpad Bogsch, the long-serving Deputy Director of BIRPI (*Bureaux Internationaux réunis pour la protection de la propriété intellectuelle*), who became the first Director General of the WIPO. The treaty finally came into force, after some years of diplomatic negotiation, in 1978.[5] Although in its first five years the administration of the PCT ran a deficit, after some revisions in procedures, it started to generate an increasing fee income, and after 1988 the number of applications administered started to expand rapidly.

At the heart of the PCT is the "international patent" that allows applicants to seek simultaneous protection in all contracting states (or a designated selection if preferred). It is important to stress that the "international patent" is not an actual patent, but rather a pre-patent that can establish the patentability of the technology or process concerned. The advantage of filing an application for an international patent through the PCT is that once the application criteria have been fulfilled there will be no subsequent requirement to amend the application for a filing in any of the jurisdictions nominated by the applicant. The PCT allows for an international examination, to ascertain the validity of the patent's fulfillment of patentability criteria, and once the "patent" is issued this acts to clearly establish priority in any national patent disputes.

National patent offices have access to all the international PCT-related search and examination reports; these are prepared by one of the major patent offices, of which the European Patent Office is the most widely used, handling over half the searches in 2004. Thus, especially for under-resourced offices in the poorer member countries of the WIPO, considerable cost-savings may be achieved through acceptance of international patent applications, not least as the PCT allows the granting of applications without a duplicated process of examination.

The PCT system does, of course, make it considerably easier for non-nationals to seek patent protection across a large number of countries without necessarily expecting to work the patent immediately in the jurisdiction. Indeed, the PCT has facilitated a rapid increase in the filing of patents by non-nationals across the developing country membership of the WIPO.[6] Perhaps most significantly, filing for an international patent under the PCT allows the applicant an 18-month window between the "priority date" that will be crucial in any dispute and the need to file for a national patent in any jurisdiction that the applicant operates in. Thus, once filed, the applicant can deploy the patent-pending technology or process without immediate concern that a valid patent has yet to be gained in that specific jurisdiction. Although applications can be filed in any language, they are required to include a translation into one of the PCT publication languages (Chinese, English, French, German, Japanese, Russian or Spanish). The PCT also established the International Patent Cooperation Union, with its own assembly, but administered by the WIPO's International Bureau. Given that the fees earned through the PCT are the WIPO's main (and crucial) income stream, it is no surprise that around half of the organization's staff work administering the PCT.

In 1990, there were 19,809 international applications filed, by 1995 this had doubled to 40,008, and had doubled again by 2000 (93,240 applications). This growth has since slackened, and while still growing, the number of applications lodged in 2004 was only around 30 percent higher than 5 years previously (at 121,264 applications). Of these applications, in 2004, around 35 percent originated in the US, while 16 percent originated in Japan and 12 percent in Germany. Thus the three leading applicant originating countries accounted for nearly two thirds of all international patent applications under the PCT. Another 12 percent was accounted for by applications from France, the United Kingdom, and the Netherlands (4.2 percent; 4.2 percent; and 3.5 percent respectively), leaving the rest of the current 124 members of the WIPO accounting for around a quarter of all applications.[7] While these proportions fluctuate over different years there is no reason to believe that 2004 was anomalous or atypical for any reason. The number of applications from developing countries is also rising; for instance from 5,861 in 2003, to 7,268 in 2004, with South Korean companies applying for almost double the number of those from China, in second place (3,553 and 1,704 respectively), and far ahead of India (667), Singapore (423), South Africa (401), Brazil (278) and Mexico (118). Of the rest only Egypt (53 applications) was the origin of more than 50 applications.[8] Thus, broadly speaking the PCT, at least currently, is a system that is mainly utilized by, and providing benefits for, corporations from a small minority of the membership of the WIPO.[9]

As well as the PCT, the WIPO also administers the Madrid system for international trademarks, which at the end of 2003 encompassed over 400,000 registered international trademarks. While the Madrid Union is still expanding, generally international marks are only registered on average in 12 of the members, but nevertheless this represents the equivalent of nearly five million national registrations.[10] Alongside these major treaties with large administrative loads, the WIPO also runs the Hague system for industrial designs, and the Lisbon system for Appellations of Origin (geographical indicators), each of which has a smaller number of members, and correspondingly represent a smaller call on the WIPO's administrative resources.[11] Although these other activities generate some income, this is dwarfed by the fee income that the PCT generates.

As G. Bruce Doern has noted, the business community has largely accepted the argument put forward by the WIPO that corporate users of the PCT and the other registrations systems have a clear interest in "ensuring that appropriate IP regimes and practices [are] present in as broad a range of countries as possible."[12] Therefore, the use of fee income from the WIPO's registration activities to support training and support for developing countries has prompted the corporations that use the WIPO's services to accept higher fees than required merely to fund administration of the PCT, the Madrid and Lisbon systems. However, in the last couple of years this consensus on fee levels has started to break down, partly because many companies from developing countries, who are now seeking international patents themselves, find the system prohibitively expensive. However, as yet this has not had a significant effect on the budget of the WIPO's non-registration activities. We now turn to these training and support activities, which are the aspect of the work of the WIPO that has most impact on the structures and practices of the contemporary global political economy.

The Co-Operation for Development Program

Although the WIPO's role in the global governance of intellectual property has been circumscribed by the establishment of the TRIPs agreement, this expansion of protection for IPRs has stimulated demand for technical support to introduce and amend national legislation to fulfill international commitments in intellectual property. Thus, under the rubric of "development co-operation" the WIPO's own pronouncements continue to emphasize that the organization's aim is

> to promote respect for intellectual property inside each developing country and in the international relations of that country, because experience shows that national creativity in the field of technical inventiveness and in the literary and artistic field is considerably enhanced, and in fact, is really only possible if it is accompanied by the protection of inventors and the authors of literary or artistic works, and if such protection extends to investors who are ready to invest in creativity.[13]

For the WIPO, development is directly tied to the recognition of IPRs, both domestically and across borders. This explicit recognition of its role regarding development is a direct consequence of the organization's status as a UN specialized agency, and the WIPO has a number of programs that help developing countries adopt modern legislation and regulation in the field of intellectual property to this end.

The WIPO "Co-operation for Development Program" has two distinct elements, an assistance program and maintenance of a documentation collection. The Collection of Laws section of the WIPO has centralized the archiving of the legislative texts which are received by the International Bureau of the WIPO. These are available electronically to all members, to aid the drafting of their own legislation; the section also publishes periodicals, distributed to members, drawing attention to aspects of the collection. The assistance program is conducted through a formal agreement with the WTO and is explicitly aimed at transitional developing countries to enable them to draft

TRIPs-compliant legislation. As the WIPO noted in their overview of the program in 2002, this assistance may take a number of forms:

> Depending on the content of the request and on the situation of the country concerned, it may take the form of the submission of a WIPO draft law on any aspect of industrial property or on copyright and related rights, or of WIPO comments or studies on draft laws prepared by the government or on existing laws as regards their compatibility with relevant international treaties . . . or any legal advice on any specific aspect of intellectual property law. *To the extent possible* the advice given takes into account the specific needs of the country concerned, in harmony with its legal, economic and political system.[14]

While members' concerns may be heeded, this can only take place within the constraints of the requirements of the agreements that states have acceded to in the field of intellectual property; broadly speaking this means that TRIPs compliance is the key element of any program of support.

This support is available to all members of the WIPO and the WTO. Draft laws and other legal instruments frequently circulate between a government legislative team and the WIPO staff a number of times before a final draft is settled on. These negotiations may also include visits to the country concerned by staff from the WIPO or invitations for key legislators and/or civil servants to Geneva for consultations. After the law has been enacted, the WIPO offers national workshops on the adopted legislation, judicial symposia and training for enforcement officers. Following a decision by the WIPO General Assembly in September 2001, a unit for developing countries was established to co-ordinate the WIPO's technical assistance activities, to ensure the non-duplication of work both within WIPO itself and also between WIPO and other agencies with which it has links, including the rest of the UN system's organizations with interests in the realm of IPRs. In addition to its work with public sector legislators, administrators and enforcement agencies, the WIPO also seeks to promote awareness in the private sector of the advantages of IPRs and the manner in which innovation and enterprise development can be supported through their use.

The aim of the WIPO's programs is to enable legislators, public sector practitioners (from judges to enforcement agencies) and also private sector actors (from patent agents to research and development executives) to develop knowledge and familiarity with the forms of intellectual property protection that their countries have committed themselves to through their membership of the WTO and/or the various treaties the WIPO oversees. With the increasingly common inclusion of IPR-related provisions in bilateral trade and investment treaties, the programs have also often been used to support non-multilateral commitments as well. Access to model and existing legal instruments helps legislators and public servants from developing countries draft domestic legislation in an area where they may have little or no national laws on which to build, and indeed may have little or no experience of current practices of regulation and protection. Additionally, the WIPO programs explicitly recognize that the establishment of laws is only the first step and therefore the organization offers considerable guidance and technical support in the realm of administration of IPR-systems and their practical enforcement.

To give an appreciation of the scale of the WIPO's technical support, and capacity building operations, between January 1998 and June 2001 the WIPO provided the following technical assistance for developing countries:

- 2,087 intellectual property officials from developing countries received training in awareness building and human resources development (1,451 from Africa, 383 from Asia-Pacific, 225 from Arabic-speaking developing countries and 28 from Haiti);
- 34 developing countries received assistance in building-up or upgrading their intellectual property offices with adequate institutional infrastructure and resources, qualified staff, modern management techniques and access to information technology support systems;
- the WIPO sponsored study visits through the WIPO Worldwide Academy for officials from the developing countries, and organized study tours for officials from many developing countries to offices in industrialized countries to study various aspects of modernization;
- 32 developing countries were beneficiaries of the WIPO assistance on legislation in the areas of intellectual property, copyright and neighboring rights and geographical indications;
- in close co-operation with other international organizations, the WIPO organized national, regional and interregional meetings for the developing countries on the implementation of the TRIPs agreement.[15]

More recently, during 2003, the WIPO reported that more than 17,000 representatives from 98 developing countries participated in

228 meetings, seminars and other training sessions, while staff of the WIPO undertook around 300 missions to developing countries to offer support and assistance in implementing various aspects of IPRs.[16] This includes: the work of various regional bureaus – the African, Arab, Asia & Pacific, Latin American & Caribbean, and Least Developed Countries' bureaus; the Office for Intellectual Property Law Development, that prepared 19 draft laws and provided legislative advice in over 3,000 cases during the period; the Office for Collective Management of Copyright and Related Rights that assisted 42 collective management societies; and the WIPO Worldwide Academy that delivered its distance learning materials to over 8,000 students from 180 countries, as well as offering various sessions to over 150 policy makers from 80 countries in the Policy Development Program.[17] The extent of this work reflects the WIPO's stated view that a "clear and balanced view of the Agreement enables the developing countries to assess the conformity of their existing national legislation vis-à-vis the provisions of the TRIPs Agreement." Thus, in line with its commitments to the UN system, the WIPO operates extensively in countries that have as yet only underdeveloped regulatory and legal practices in place.

The WIPO in the World of TRIPs

In the last decade of the twentieth century international trade diplomacy finally established a global regime for the governance of IPRs: the TRIPs agreement. In many ways the TRIPs agreement, like much of the previous history of the governance of IPRs, was a response to technological changes as well as political economic shifts.[18] However, the TRIPs agreement was also part of a more general settlement among the crucial regional trading blocs, in the wake of the end of the Cold War, that the governance of international trade should move from the relatively weak General Agreement on Tariffs and Trade to a new and more robust governance regime. The inclusion of TRIPs, alongside the General Agreement on Trade in Services (GATS), and a number of other agreements, ranging from investment to antidumping, into the final settlement of the Uruguay Round of multilateral trade negotiations was the culmination of a general strategy on behalf of the US government and the European Union to force developing countries to adopt multilateral agreements in sectors which they had hitherto resisted.[19] By withdrawing from their previous commitments under GATT 1947, and therefore terminating any obligations under that agreement, the US and EU forced developing countries to accede to a wide-ranging agreement under the WTO if they wished to regain the trade arrangements with which they had started the Uruguay Round.

The TRIPs agreement presents WTO members with a single framework for dealing with the diverse aspects of intellectual property. It is not a model piece of legislation that can be incorporated directly into national law, but rather sets the minimum standards to be established by all WTO members. National legislatures are required to ensure that IPRs are protected, but the method for this protection is only important as regards its consequences, not its form; the agreement is concerned with ends, not means. However, unlike the WIPO's stewardship of the major conventions that have now been largely incorporated into the TRIPs agreement, governing IPRs through the WTO offers a considerably more robust mechanism for countries' governments to appeal to when the laws of a particular country are seen to impede the rights of other nationals.

Crucially, and unlike other aspects of WTO members' undertakings, the TRIPs agreement is a set of requirements for *positive* legislative action to establish the rights and protections mandated by its various articles, rather than merely requiring states to refrain from certain actions or practices. The history of domestic political deliberation has produced varied and locally determined solutions to the question of making knowledge and information property, but this is not merely undermined by the agreement, it is explicitly replaced by a set of standards that have (for most countries) been developed elsewhere. Therefore, the establishment of TRIPs represented a major shift from the variable regime favored by the WIPO, replacing it with a more robustly governed, multilateral regime that set a "floor" to the protection of IPRs.

The keystone of the TRIPs agreement is the application to intellectual property of the principles that are central to the WTO, like the GATT before it: national treatment; most-favored nation treatment (MFN); and reciprocity. Reciprocity as a principle does little in itself to change the intellectual property regime as the agreements previously overseen by the WIPO were negotiated on this basis. However, the combination of MFN and national treatment ensures that the previous favoritism accorded domestic inventors or prospective owners of IPRs relative to non-nationals is rendered illegal, as is the favorable treatment of IPR-owners from specific trading partners; in the past many national IPR systems favored domestic "owners" either through legislative or procedural means. Therefore, although the character of intellectual property, what is actually to be protected, is modified to some extent by the TRIPs agreement, especially for computer programs, the main area of discontinuity with prior practice is in the national protection of IPRs. If only nationals are protected this acts as a barrier to non-nationals who receive no protection for the IPR-related goods or services they wish to export to that jurisdiction. Non-discrimination must be explicitly part of clear, open and fair procedures for the protection of IPRs.

In the text of the TRIPs agreement the recognition that IPRs were to be conceived as "private rights" was partly balanced by an explicit allowance of the need for the "public policy objectives" to be accorded some weight in regard of both developmental and technological objectives. However, the agreement clearly focuses on extending owners' rights. Indeed, Kurt Burch contends that this expansion of ownership rights "promotes the vocabulary of rights and property and the liberal conceptual framework they help define."[20] For knowledge and information this leads to the emphasis on *individualized* rights to reward for effort, alongside the practical organization of production through alienable property. Furthermore, Samuel Oddi argues that the use of a natural *rights* discourse is intended to establish that

> these rights are so important that individual [WTO] member welfare should not stand in the way of their being protected as an entitlement of the creators. This invokes a counter-instrumentalist policy that members, regardless of their state of industrialization, should sacrifice their national interests in favor of the posited higher order of international trade.[21]

While the TRIPs agreement includes instrumentalist justifications alongside the more rights-oriented language, throughout the text the agreement systematically privileges the rights side of any balance between individual rights and public development benefits.

Likewise the widespread use of the term "piracy" by negotiators before and after the TRIPs negotiations is symbolic of this set of naturalized claims, implying that infringers should be thought of like the pirates, slave traders and torturers of the past.[22] This is a rhetorical attempt to establish the parallel with more violent assaults on human rights, despite the fact, as Howard Anawalt notes, that IPRs "lack the compelling necessity of human rights covenants or rules on the use of force."[23] However, this rhetoric of "rights" continues to be a powerful aspect of the agreement's normative commitments, and is a major element in the WIPO's activities as regards its programs to widen and underpin support for the protection of IPRs in the contemporary global political economy. Indeed, while the TRIPs agreement may offer methods of enforcement, the explicit partnership between the WTO and the WIPO is intended to allow the latter to ensure that enforcement by the former does not have to be relied upon.

Thus, while the TRIPs agreement itself is a complex and wide-ranging set of requirements on signatories,[24] at the core is a particular set of norms regarding the treatment of knowledge as property. These norms underpin the entire agreement and are based on the notion that the private ownership of knowledge as property is a major spur to continued economic development and social welfare. These norms further emphasize that the development of knowledge is an individual-ized endeavor, and that the legitimate reward of such individualized effort is intellectual property. Most obviously this includes a robust norm of commodification of knowledge and information. While the agreement is potentially quite flexible, as evidenced by the negotia-tions over the Doha Declaration on the TRIPs Agreement and Public Health at the WTO (November 2001), the social forces that support a particular, rights emphasizing, reading of the agreement are difficult to overcome. The Doha Declaration itself, despite extensive negotia-tions at the WTO *only* reasserted the broad thrust of the TRIPs agreement's original invocation of health emergencies as legitimate reasons for the compulsory licensing of pharmaceuticals. Although the WIPO is formally quite separate from the discussions around the Doha Declaration, nevertheless it spends much of its considerable resources on underpinning and expanding the reach of the norms that are solidi-fied in the TRIPs agreement and that were reconfirmed by the declaration.

Although the TRIPs agreement carries the normal provisions regarding the criteria for patenting forward (newness, usefulness and applicability) it does not expressly preclude a considerable expansion of "patentable subject matter." This extension is produced through the provisions of article 27 which allow that members *may* exclude from patent provisions a number of classes of goods and materials, such as diagnostic, therapeutic and surgical methods as well as plants and animals, and the "essentially" biological processes for their production. These classes of objects and processes may be excluded, but they are not *required* to be outside patent regimes, and certainly in the last decade industrialized countries' governments have deployed consider-able bilateral pressure to ensure that developing countries' new TRIPs-compliant legislation covers certain new "products." These issues have now moved back to the WIPO with the discussions over the establishment of a Substantive Patent Law Treaty (SPLT) led by a number of the most developed country members of the WIPO.

The TRIPs agreement widened and strengthened what had been a much weaker governance regime overseen by the WIPO. The TRIPs agreement's most significant elements have been: firstly to bring all members of the WTO under the same set of principles and minimum standards for the recognition and protection of IPRs; secondly to give this governance regime "teeth" by applying the WTO's dispute settlement mechanism to any international disputes regarding the undertakings within TRIPs; and thirdly, by linking IPRs to the wider issues of international trade at the WTO it has made significant inroads into the hitherto sovereign ability of countries to establish, govern and regulate IPRs in response to perceived national political economic priorities. This represents a major watershed in the international history of intellectual property, but the establishment of a globalized regime of governance has also revealed some serious problems and disputes. Although a significant and important moment in the governance of IPRs, the TRIPs agreement has engendered considerable contestation and the (global) politics of IPRs have become more fraught in the last decade since the agreement became international law with the establishment of the WTO.

Although the TRIPs agreement was a direct and forthright political response to the manner in which the WIPO was deemed to be failing by the office of the USTR (Office of the United States Trade Representative) and the large US-based corporations that were influential as regards IPR-related policy, the agreement still envisaged a major role for the WIPO in the global governance of intellectual property. Indeed the formal agreement between the WTO and the WIPO that came into force on 1 January 1996 very clearly established the division of labor that has underpinned the continued effectiveness of the WIPO as an international organization. While disputes between WTO members are handled by the WTO, the agreement established a clearly defined role for the WIPO focussed on *technical* support for developing countries, as identified by the WTO. In one sense this removed the formal political dimension from the WIPO's operations, although its operations, despite claims to the contrary, remain highly politicized.

The agreement between the WTO and the WIPO established the rights of WTO members, including those that were not members of the WIPO, to access the WIPO's extensive historical records and databases of existing national laws for the governance and enforcement of intellectual property (article 2). This included a clearly defined undertaking by the WIPO to provide technical support for monitoring of the TRIPs agreement, and to support the dispute resolution mechanism through the provision of materials relevant to any particular dispute. Likewise the WTO undertook to provide all relevant documentation and legal agreements for intellectual property conducted under its auspices for open access through the WIPO's document collection system.

The agreement formally empowered the WIPO to oversee the registration and governance of national emblems, and their use in international trade (article 3), but, perhaps most importantly given the WIPO's subsequent role in supporting the establishment of TRIPs-compliant laws in developing countries, the WIPO was, and continues to be obliged to offer technical assistance to *any* developing country member of the WTO in relation to intellectual property laws (article 4). This is a reciprocal arrangement, with the WTO also undertaking to make available to any developing countries that are currently not members of the WTO the same technical assistance made available to members. To this end formal lines of communication between the two organizations were opened and have allowed the support available to developing countries in the realm of intellectual property to be fully co-ordinated.

In recognition of its role in the implementation of the TRIPs agreement, the developed country members of the WIPO, led by the US and the EU, have increased their budget contributions to facilitate the capacity building and legislative advice functions of the organization. The WIPO's inability to offer the robust and effective methods of dispute resolution that were introduced by the WTO has now been turned into an advantage in the division of labor between the two institutions. The consensual, and variable speed approach of the WIPO, allowing states to join agreements facilitated by the WIPO when their negotiators recognize a national interest in doing so, has enabled the International Bureau to broker a number of sets of negotiations leading to new intellectual property-related treaties. Thus while the WTO works slowly to establish consensual agreements among the entire membership, the WIPO can act to initiate treaties and agreements between willing sub-groups that can in time become more generally acceded to. This inter-institutional synergy has allowed the organizations to enter "a symbiotic relationship that takes advantage of the strengths of each."[25] Indeed in a sense, this division of tasks and the shift to a more specialized role within the governance regime has prompted the WIPO to become more rather than less active.

This renewed activity has established what Laurence Hefler has termed a "normative feedback loop in the WTO, influencing both TRIPs dispute settlement and member states' proposals to amend or supplement TRIPs."[26] Therefore, the WIPO has maintained significant influence over the shape and direction of further developments in the global governance of IPRs. However, now that the WIPO's pre-TRIPs monopoly has been broken, and perhaps reflecting the increased global awareness of the impact of the regulation and enforcement of IPRs, disputes about the direction of further developments in the governance of intellectual property are being raised in a number of other venues; for instance, in discussions over the Convention on Bio-Diversity since its establishment in 1992, at the Food and Agricultural Organization, at the World Health Organization, and across numerous other members of the UN system.[27] Thus, it is no surprise that while the WIPO has managed to remain extraordinarily active in the realm of IPRs, this has not been easy nor without its own troubles. As we will see in the next two chapters, the WIPO's continuing attempts to maintain its role in the global governance of IPRs have opened up the organization to new criticism.

4 Global Governance and Intellectual Property

As the new millennium unfolds, the analysis and evaluation of global governance continues to expand both in policy making circles and in universities across the world. While much of the post-Westphalian history of the international system has been a story of inter-state relations and conflict, since 1945 the move towards a more multilateral governance system has gathered momentum, especially since the end of the Cold War in 1989. The origins of much that is now discussed under the rubric of global governance can be traced back at least to the first flowering of international organization in the mid to late nineteenth century,[1] and likewise the World Intellectual Property Organization finds its roots in this period, but the idea of the possibility of global governance is of more recent vintage.

The contemporary idea of global governance seeks to capture something more than the multilateral co-ordination of state activities through the membership of issue-specific organizations. Rather, global governance identifies the emergence and development of political leadership by these organizations, moving beyond their mere enacting of state governmental instructions and interests. Although no international organization has complete autonomy from, and power over, its members, few international organizations remain only agents of state power. Discussions of global governance try to capture the ability of organizations to set the pace and agenda of governance over specific issues at the supra-state level, while also accepting that state sovereignty still looms large in any calculation of the manner in which the global system is governed. The WIPO itself is an excellent example of this balance between organizational leadership and the limitations on actions that are prompted by member states' sovereignty and the continuing articulation of national interests.

Despite the political pressure from various states, and the re-orientation of the global governance of intellectual property rights since the conclusion of the Uruguay Round, the WIPO has remained active in three key areas. The WIPO has retained its role in the international application and registration regimes; it has also expanded its activities in the area of technical assistance and capacity building; and, it has renewed its role in the development of new multilateral governance mechanisms for specific realms of intellectual property. Thus, rather than suffering a loss of competence due to forum shopping as has often been suggested, the WIPO has more accurately fought to maintain its position during a period of forum proliferation. The multilateral governance of intellectual property has become more complex and multi-faceted as governance more generally has become more globalized, but the WIPO has striven to maintain its position and importance. Thus, in this chapter we shall examine three aspects of the WIPO's current activities to ascertain how successful it has been in maintaining a role in global governance, but this also starts to reveal the problems this strategy has involved.

One of the key problems that the development of the Internet presented to owners of intellectual property was the interaction between international trademarks and domain names. Here the WIPO's work with the Internet Corporation for Assigned Names and Numbers (ICANN) is illustrative of how the WIPO has used its diplomatic experience to carve out a role in emerging issue areas. The WIPO has also worked with a number of organizations to deliver various forms of technical assistance to countries working to fulfill their international obligations as regards intellectual property, and these activities will be examined to identify some key difficulties that will be taken up in the final chapters. Finally we examine some of the new treaties that the WIPO has managed to broker, and look at the continuing negotiations it hosts. All of these activities underline how successful the WIPO has been at maintaining a role for itself in the global governance of intellectual property.

The WIPO and ICANN: The Problem of Trademarks on the Internet

Due to the expansion of interest in intellectual property in the last decades, in addition to the World Trade Organization (WTO) a number of other agencies and non-state actors have had, and continue to have, dealings with the WIPO over specific issues. The difficulties some of the development-oriented United Nations specialized agencies have encountered will be discussed in the next chapter; here, the WIPO's relationship with the ICANN will be a useful example of the manner in which inter-agency interactions have been developed, especially when the ends concern the extension and protection of already established intellectual property rights (IPRs).[2] Moreover, as Frederick Abbot has pointed out, this is an excellent example of the manner in which the WIPO has moved beyond the passive secretariat model in international organizations, to one that is much more proactive.[3]

The WIPO has worked with ICANN to establish a mechanism for ameliorating the "problem" of domain name allocation in relation to trademarks, although this was also part of a longer process of further expanding the international protection available to trademark owners. In 1999 the WIPO Assembly adopted a Resolution Concerning Provisions on the Protection of Well-Known Marks, and the following year approved a Recommendation Concerning Trademark Licenses. Then in 2001, a Recommendation Concerning Provisions on the Protection of Marks and Other Industrial Property Rights in Signs, on the Internet was adopted.[4] These three agreements, while not formal treaties, were intended to work towards establishing specific norms regarding the protection of trademarks as part of the wider "soft law initiative" at the WIPO that underpins much of the organization's activities since the establishment of the Trade Related Aspects of Intellectual Property Rights (TRIPs) agreement. These agreements followed extensive lobbying by the private sector, whose representatives asked the WIPO to examine the problems with international trademark protection resulting from the expansion of the Internet. It is clear that the WIPO was therefore not only driven by the interests of its members, but regarded the private sector's concerns in this area as a legitimate subject for organizational attention.

By virtue of the domain name system around which the Internet was (and continues to be) organized, once a domain name has been assigned, this name has an international practical validity. The key issue for owners of internationally renowned marks was to ensure that the domain name was assigned to them. Prior to the establishment of any global governance regime for domain names, the principle for allocation had been essentially "first come, first served."[5] The system of allocating domains emerged from early discussions among users of "domain requirements"; the major top-level domains (.gov; .edu; .com; .mil; and .org), alongside the two-letter country domains (.uk; .ch; .fr, and so on) that are still in use today were set out in a document by Jon Postel and Joyce Reynolds in 1984.[6] As the use of the Internet accelerated in the 1990s however, the relatively simple administration of domain name allocation started to buckle under the demand for names, disputes over allocations, and domain names' relation to already existing trademarks.

In the early years of the Internet, one well-known money-making scheme was to apply for, and have assigned, a domain name that was also a well-known brand or trademark, and then offer to sell this domain-name to the trademark owner, often referred to as "cyber-squatting."[7] Unsurprisingly, many trademark holders regarded this as at best sharp practice, and at worst as blackmail. This problem was finally resolved by the adoption by the ICANN of the Uniform Domain Name Dispute Resolution Policy (UDRP, 1999), developed with the WIPO. This agreement mediates disputes regarding owner-ship of trade names when used as internet addresses, ensuring that trademarked names are "correctly" assigned.

In 1993, when Network Solutions Inc. (NSI) was contracted by the US National Science Foundation to manage the domain name process, it was making around 400 registrations a month; however by September 1996, this had risen to 80,000 registrations a month,[8] and it has expanded exponentially since. The interaction of national trade-mark registration and the global scope of domain names created a significant problem of misalignment between trademark rights and the possibility of utilizing them for commercial advantage. Unsurprisingly, trademark owners were adamant that if the Internet was increasingly a globalized commercial space, then trademark regu-lation needed to be conducted across the same realm.[9] However, the NSI's policy of suspending any domain name on the receipt of a complaint by a trademark owner also generated widespread criticism.[10] Therefore, to establish a more equitable dispute settlement procedure, a number of arenas including the UN and the International Telecommunications Union were considered by various commenta-tors,[11] before the WIPO was able to assert its competence to broker a solution to the problem.

The US government to a large extent drove the reform of the domain name system, once it became clear that a consensus in line with US interests was unlikely to emerge spontaneously through the private sector's efforts. Thus in 1997 the US government, emphasizing the commercial issue of trademark misuse, and after a period of often fraught consultation and international lobbying, initiated a formal process of consultation, that the following year led to the establishment of ICANN as a non-profit corporation to take over the responsibility for allocating domain names and a number of other duties.

Alongside this process, the WIPO itself was invited to develop proposals both for the management of a system that would encompass trademarks, and the development of a dispute settlement mecha-nism.[12] Although in some respects a rather ambiguous policy process,

Graeme Dinwoodie argues that essentially the WIPO "acted at the request of a single member state (the United States) to produce a report that, by virtue of delegation of de facto control of the domain name registration process from the single government, could be implemented by ICANN as substantive law without the usual airings found in intergovernmental lawmaking of which WIPO is a part."[13] Although the WIPO did circulate the proposals for comments, because this was outside their standard intergovernmental practice, and also as the Uniform Dispute Resolution Policy (UDRP) can be contradicted in national courts, the anomalous character of the procedure has not prompted a major shift away from previous policy, or a repetition of this process for other issues. Conversely, it *does* suggest that the WIPO does not merely operate on the basis of the clearly articulated interest of a *majority* of its members.

While the ICANN adopted most of the WIPO's proposals for the UDRP, it also included some amendments reflecting concerns that some aspects of the policy did not recognize individual and non-commercial uses, and free speech defenses for "infringement," as well as some other more technical issues that had been raised during consultation. Indeed, to some extent the WIPO's proposals had too clearly revealed that the private sector and the WIPO saw the ICANN process as a way of extending and consolidating the power and advantage of trademark owners over the Internet.[14] However, most importantly the WIPO was not the only provider of dispute resolution services in the resulting system: it was joined by the National Arbitration Forum (NAF) and the Disputes.org/eResolution Consortium.[15] Under the UDRP the choice between these services usually reflected an assessment by the complainant of the forum most likely to get the decision they required.

The process was intended to deliver swift judgments on disputes. Complainants needed to demonstrate that the name is identical or confusingly similar; that the current holder does not retain rights or have legitimate interests in the domain name itself; and that the domain name holder is using the name in bad faith. However, the ICANN has also established three defenses to these charges that are acceptable in the process of complaint: that the domain name is being used in business in good faith; that the registrant of the domain name was already known by this name, even if no trademark had been issued; or where a fair use or non-commercial use can be demonstrated.[16] Thus, like the other service providers, here the WIPO was (and is) merely providing a service based on its diplomatic and technical expertise.

Early indications were that the WIPO and NAF arbitration panels were the most complainant friendly, and most likely to privilege trademark owners' interests, while the eResolution Consortium was more defendant friendly, and seemed to apply the UDRP more neutrally.[17] However, with the dissolution of the eResolution service due to a lack of business, which tells us something about the character of the majority of the disputes, the balance of advantage swung further towards trademark holders. Indeed, the WIPO panel has also allowed surname and geographic name holders to bring successful complaints against domain name registrants,[18] despite the seemingly clear fair use defenses that registrants of such domains might use according to the UDRP. Here the WIPO's traditional users have again been favored over Internet start-ups and recent entrants to the realm of IPRs.

This competition between arbitration services also reveals that the UDRP is what has become known as "soft law," a process that is a hybrid between ministerial, judicial and arbitrational governance.[19] It is here, in a realm where rules and governance are dependent as much on reputation and imputed normative value, as they are on formalized legal undertakings, that the WIPO with its established diplomatic record, and clear links with the private sector through its other activities (primarily, but not exclusively, the Patent Co-operation Treaty) is able to gain some advantage.

The WIPO systematically approached national domain registries, that govern the country-coded top-level domains like .uk, offering them help with disputes.[20] Additionally, once the balance of decisions became well known, it is also perhaps of little surprise that the trademark holders, often the more assiduous complainants, moved to the forum most likely to favor them, producing a loss of business for eResolution, and their withdrawal from the service. In May 2003, the WIPO's arbitrations center received its 5,000th UDRP case, and during that year arbitration requests were being received at a rate of just under 1,000 requests a month.[21]

Finally, although this system remains dominated by the US, not least as ICANN remains a contractor for the US Department of Commerce, there is increasing disquiet about the influence this gives the US government over the Internet. Not only developing countries but also the European Union have sought to establish a more multinational governance regime. However, although these disputes are important, and were greatly exercised at the World Information Society summit in Tunis in November 2005, there is as yet little sign of such complaints prompting a major shift in the system. If any new governing body moved to change the dispute resolution system, and this may be the result of the Internet Governance Forum that was launched after much dispute and debate at the Tunis summit, the WIPO would be likely to once again capitalize on its reputation and diplomatic expertise to remain near the center of any revised arrangements. However, such a change does not look imminent given the intransigence of the US government over this issue.

As Edward Kwakwa reminds us, "political commitment often plays a vital role in international law,"[22] and certainly the WIPO has continued to be committed to the governance of IPRs, despite some attempts to sideline it in favor of other organizations. As we have seen in the case of Internet domain names, by establishing its expertise, and delivering resolution services that have been advantageous to IPR-owners, the WIPO has managed to maintain its position in the international realm of intellectual property. However, this has also been supported by a major campaign to establish a supportive environment for its operations, and it is the manner in which this has been achieved that we move to next.

Technical Assistance, Capacity Building and the (Re)Production of the TRIPs Mindset

Formally responding to its commitments to the WTO, but also building on its previous activities and expertise, the WIPO has expanded its technical assistance and capacity building programs in the last decade. Mostly this has been focussed on those developing countries struggling to fulfill their international commitments as regards national legislation to protect IPRs.[23] Although some governments' doubts about the usefulness of IPRs for lesser developed countries are sometimes acknowledged by the WIPO's staff, mostly these are swiftly dismissed in its publications and materials; officially the WIPO *promotes* the establishment of law and institutions for the regulation and protection of intellectual property.[24]

As Sisule Musungu and Graham Dutfield have argued: "what [the] WIPO can do is limited by its institutional orientations, political considerations and other limitations. This in itself should not be a problem. Problems arrive when [the] WIPO fails to acknowledge its limitations."[25] Indeed, perhaps the most obvious overall limitation that the WIPO is constrained by is its own focus on IPRs as an absolute social good, allowing issues of economic development only a secondary place in any assessment of the forms of technical assistance that might be appropriate in any specific case. Thus, in the WIPO's programs the stage of development (for want of a better term) is discounted as an indicator of the appropriate forms of protection for intellectual property in any particular country. Essentially, the WIPO has developed and promotes a "one-size-fits-all" solution; its technical assistance is intended to deliver this "solution" to those countries without fully functioning intellectual property systems. Technical assistance and capacity building programs aim to help countries re-orient national legal regimes in line with the TRIPs agreement's provisions when they have no domestic tradition and expertise in the field of intellectual property, or if their legislative experience is different from the TRIPs model.

Unfortunately, the western notion of IPRs does not closely reflect customary practice in many developing countries, or often more accurately, the lack of any established practice. Without such support, legal innovation can be relatively difficult to sustain. As Graeme Dinwoodie notes: "It is economic and social contexts that *sustain* these laws [of intellectual property], and if a similar social setting does not exist, merely harmonizing [legal] texts may be of little value."26 As this implies, the WIPO programs therefore have not merely been about providing model legislation for developing countries, and assessing their proposed laws, but rather have just as importantly been about socializing policy makers into valuing and supporting the protection of IPRs. Thus, technical assistance is not merely important in the aid it provides governments and legislators with to establish specific legislation, but is also an important political, or even ideological, program of social re-orientation.

As members of the WTO, or as prospective members, many countries' governments find themselves needing to adopt laws that have little familiarity, or to which some elements of society *and* the government may be hostile. The requirements of the TRIPs agreement are compounded by the fact that many countries, having entered into bilateral agreements with one or more of the major IPR-exporting countries, also find themselves under significant pressure to swiftly put in place further expanded protection for IPRs. The Office of the US Trade Representative (USTR) has access to what has been described as "a global surveillance network, consisting of American companies, the American Chamber of Commerce, trade associations and American embassies, a network that gathers and reports on the minutiae of [countries'] social and legal practices when it comes to US intellectual property."27 The USTR uses the information this network provides to bring considerable political pressure to bear on those countries regarded as laggards in protecting US industries' intellectual property. Seeking to comply, at least minimally, with these demands for political and legal change, policy makers in developing countries have responded well to the WIPO's advances as regards assistance and education. They have become willing participants in the programs, both in their own countries, and those which are carried out in Geneva where attendance may have other attractions as well.

Although the TRIPs agreement does not actually mandate the forms of law that any member must adopt, as Michael Finger and Philip Schuler have concluded the tendency is

> to give the benefit of the doubt to established standards. Finding grounds for moving away from established standards may be particularly difficult in the area of intellectual property rights. They are, after all, an existential matter of legal definition, not a scientific matter of empirical estimation . . . [Thus] the benefit of the doubt will rest with systems presently in place in the industrialized countries.[28]

This is to say that the technical assistance and capacity building programs that the WIPO operates do not support novel or different solutions to the problems of IPR protection. Rather, any countries' specific circumstances are only likely to be accorded any weight in the programs where this does not conflict with the TRIPs agreement's invocation of required legal effect, and the "best practice" acknowledged by the WIPO and the various other agencies involved in capacity building programs. However, where prior legal culture and the TRIPs-compliant laws come into conflict it is by no means certain that the new laws will be regarded as legitimate in wider society. Here the WIPO's socialization of policy makers becomes very important; training and education can produce advocates in domestic policy elites for the new and/or changed protection of IPRs and this may help overcome local objections, even if it is often impossible to silence them.

Despite the enactment of a legal framework that is broadly TRIPs-compliant, supported by capacity building projects, enforcement practices may also remain underdeveloped. Indeed, without clear cultural support legislation will be seen merely as the imposition of foreign laws by distant policy elites. However, where economic development stimulates the emergence of an industrial constituency which is likely to support stronger protection, then capacity building may find more fertile ground. As well as producing a wide range of public information material on the value of patents to help support these emergent constituencies in developing countries, the WIPO has a Small and Medium-Sized Enterprises division that works with various agencies to support companies in their use of IPRs, thereby encouraging their political demands for legislation where none exists or where it is insufficiently enforced. In 2003, in addition to work with companies in the OECD countries, for instance, the SME division worked with the Confederation of Indian Industry and a number of chambers of commerce in developing countries, as well as commissioning studies with local partners on "the need for SMEs to make more effective use of the IP system."[29] The demand for this support will be related to the relative global position of the sector concerned: a thriving content sector in a developing country may be more receptive to TRIPs compliance than a relatively underdeveloped pharmaceutical sector.

The WIPO has expended considerable political effort to (re)produce the globalized norms that are at the heart of the TRIPs agreement. Law cannot work if it is only followed when there is continual explicit enforcement, and thus it is crucial that the recognition of its precepts is socially embedded; a complete lack of embeddedness will be fatal to any law. This is even more the case where the law itself disturbs the common character of that which it regulates; in this case through the commodification of previously "free" knowledge and/or information. Thus, while the possession of material goods, and the provision of personal services may be protected, or access and use withheld by force, this is not the case for knowledge and information made property. In the absence of socially accepted IPRs, it is difficult to govern access to knowledge and information unless it is kept altogether secret. Few if any knowledge-related businesses can expect to thrive without revealing the knowledge/informational base of their products or services. Therefore, when the required commodification of knowledge is not seen as legitimate, it is very difficult to establish markets for knowledge or information-related products or services.

In light of developing countries' different legal histories, and their divergent interests, especially as related to the OECD countries, in many cases the WIPO's programs are crucial to shift perceptions of the value of legislating for intellectual property's protection. Certainly, the current settlement for IPRs may work well for the developed countries' industries, but for many developing countries the central bargain between private rewards and public benefits at the center of IPRs often makes little sense. The private rights of IPR "owners" in the richer states are being purchased at what to many in the developing countries seems too great a social cost. To shift perceptions the WIPO has had to work hard, reflecting what Stephen Gill calls a wider political dynamic of the "new constitutionalism"; an attempt "to make transnational liberalism, and if possible liberal democratic capitalism, the sole model for future development."[30] While the global governance of IPRs is only one, albeit important, part of this "project," its contours are clearly discernible.

The TRIPs-mandated settlement on governance of intellectual property stresses and privileges the rights and needs of knowledge "owners" while removing from the public realm substantial knowledge and information resources. As Gill suggests, under this new constitutionalism "public policy is increasingly premised on the goal of increasing security of property (owners) and minimizing the uncertainty of investors."[31] In policy terms, the "new constitutionalism" stresses the "need to strengthen surveillance mechanisms, and institutional capabilities to reinforce . . . market discipline at the multilateral level, and to help to sustain the legal and political conditions for transnational capital."[32] Thus the surveillance of the USTR and the technical assistance from the WIPO are intended to work together to ensure the world is safe for the information and knowledge suffused modern capitalism that has developed in the richest countries in the last decades.

The education of elites has also gone some way to reducing the resistance to the establishment of mechanisms of IPR regulation by two clear means. Firstly, the WIPO's programs aim to socialize policy makers, legislators and civil servants from countries with weak or absent records in enacting protection for IPRs. Secondly, after linking the protection of IPRs to international trade through the TRIPs agreement, and investment through the panoply of bilateral treaties signed in recent years by developing countries, the WIPO's technical assistance programs have reduced the effort and expertise needed to fulfill one part of a complex bargain of market entry and development through international trade that is valued by many developing country elites. Therefore, the WIPO's Co-operation for Development Program acts through socialization and technical facilitation to establish the political context in which the governance of IPRs can flourish, and to make a specific form of governance easier.

The WIPO has recognized the importance of socially embedding the governance of intellectual property in the policy elite of the developing countries, as well as the need for a more general normative reorientation. Moreover, the WIPO's work in this area has contributed to the maintenance of the organization's centrality to the global governance of intellectual property in the post-TRIPs era. However, it has not given up its more formal role in the initiation of negotiations about further enhancing the governance structures that build on the "floor" for protection established by the TRIPs agreement, and it is to this third area of activities that we now turn.

Working to Expand the Global Governance of Intellectual Property

Although the role of the WTO in the global governance of intellectual property has now been firmly established, a core group of developed countries has moved back to the WIPO to negotiate further IPR-related treaties, not so much due to forum shopping as by a process of forum proliferation. This was at least partly a result of a sustained campaign by the WIPO itself to return the organization to the center of global intellectual property policy making, but also a case of the developed countries' governments seeking a forum for negotiations where their own interests could be furthered with least resistance. Even while the Uruguay Round of multilateral trade negotiations continued, the WIPO had already begun to establish an expansive agenda of harmonization intended to raise the global standards of protection (and enforcement) of IPRs above those about to be set by TRIPs. Rather than accept that the TRIPs agreement was a final settlement in the realm of IPRs, recognizing the likely dynamic in the private sector, the WIPO seized its chance to argue for the TRIPs as a basic global standard, on which further expansions and advances in the global protection of IPRs could be based.

As part of the periodic revision process for the Berne Convention, the WIPO had in 1989 been asked by Berne's governing body to convene a committee of experts to examine how the convention might be revised in light of the advance of digital technologies.[33] To a large extent this process was driven by the US government's representation of the interests of the content and software industries based in America. Although the US negotiators did not achieve all their aims, most of their demands were met in one way or another; for instance, database protection was removed from the initial discussions, but was successfully reintroduced later. The negotiations culminated in a diplomatic conference in 1996 where the WIPO Copyright Treaty (WCT) was adopted.

Perhaps most significantly, the WCT introduced digital rights management (DRM), and crucially the anti-circumvention principle, into the multilateral governance of IPRs.[34] The introduction of DRM is intended to safeguard the rights of intellectual property owners, and recognizing that technological fixes are seldom permanent, the WCT sought to establish a further legal layer of protection for these technologies themselves. This attempted to ensure that any attempt to bypass the DRM systems encoded in digitally distributed IPR-related goods or services would be illegal, in addition to any actual rights infringement; without legal protection from tampering any DRM was essentially useless. This legal innovation was subsequently enacted in the US Digital Millennium Copyright Act (DMCA) and the EU Copyright Directive. The other key element of the WCT was to clarify and make explicit rights holders' right to make works available; while previously the right of communication had been fragmentary and unwieldy, the WCT consolidated this right to ensure it fully covered the making of works available over the Internet.[35] In essence the WCT provides the right to communicate, and thus the right to *halt* communication of the work, that had been left rather weak under the TRIPs agreement.

The WIPO Performances and Phonograms Treaty (WPPT), adopted in the same year, considerably extended the rights available to performers, from those set out in the Rome Convention or the TRIPs agreement, thus bringing them up to the level previously only enjoyed by producers. The WPPT sets out clear and exclusive rights of reproduction and distribution, including a "rental right" establishing the secondary rights over subsequent usage of digitized products. Additionally, and for the first time in international law, the WPPT established performers' moral rights over their creations, although the WPPT itself offers no guidance on what might be acceptable modifications to performances (i.e. remixing for broadcast, perhaps) and unacceptable infringements of this right of integrity.[36] Like the WCT, the WPPT also explicitly sets out the right to communicate and the protection of the technologies making up DRM. Interestingly, the treaty also expands the notion of performer to include those who perform "expressions of folklore" (article 2.a), and as such goes a little way to recognizing the concerns of developing country negotiators as regards the products of their, as yet only partially commodified, traditional culture.

Both the WCT and WPPT further extended the rights of IP owners, even as the TRIPs agreement started to attract significant criticism. Both treaties responded to a similar set of demands for the control of content linked to new forms of technological reproduction, distribution and communications, primarily linked to the expansion of the Internet. For Jörg Reinbothe and Silke von Lewinski these treaties should not be merely regarded as the WIPO's "Internet treaties" because in fact they are "equally relevant, and even crucial, for the traditional environment of exploitation of copyright and neighboring rights."

Furthermore, they effectively update the Berne and Rome conventions in their relevant areas, as well as moving the TRIPs system further in the field of copyright.[37] Taken together these treaties expanded the possibilities of commercial exploitation of IPRs by ensuring they are better protected and enforced.

As the WIPO was perceived by many private interests as having failed to fully support these sorts of rights during the period prior to the establishment of the TRIPs agreement, to return itself to the center of the global governance of intellectual property the WIPO needed to demonstrate that it understood and could react to the demands of the major knowledge industries, and their supporters. Therefore it should be no surprise that these agreements were not developed with the interest of performers or "creatives" at the forefront of consideration, but rather were intended to ensure that copyright *owners* could both consolidate and expand their rights in the realm of Internet-mediated communication.

The renewed vigor of policy making at the WIPO also led to the establishment of the WIPO Patent Agenda, and the subsequent process of consultation.[38] However, despite the WIPO formally being a membership organization, there has been a growing concern among some developing countries' representatives and other interested parties that the Director General and the International Bureau of the WIPO are working to their own agenda, one that is informed by the interests and demands of a small group of members and a number of industry groups.[39] Rather than focus on development or the wider global social interest, many critics suspect that the WIPO is privileging the interests of private owners of IPRs relative to other interests that ought to be factored in to the governance of intellectual property.

At the center of the Patent Agenda is the perceived need to develop a "universal patent," a fully globalized and harmonized patent regime, building on the international application procedure already existing under the Patent Co-operation Treaty (PCT). Indeed, if the PCT could be further extended, the likely result would be a further concentration of power over the patent process in Geneva, and the dominant patent offices, that undertake the majority of the examinations, again supporting the WIPO's continued role in global governance. However, the process of discussing the Patent Agenda has revealed some very clear areas of tension between the developed country and developing country members of the WIPO, as well as between the developed countries themselves. Because the Patent Agenda aims to remove those areas of national self-determination regarding patents that remain in the minimum standards set by TRIPs, this intention now confronts differences between the developed countries themselves.

The 2002 report by the UK Commission on IPRs presented the problem in this area as being between a policy focussing on quantity of patents, versus one that would focus on the *quality* of patent grants:

> The ever-expanding demand for patents is regarded as a right which has to be met by increasing the productivity of the granting process at the expense of a possible further reduction in quality. [The Commissioners] believe that policy makers in both developed and developing countries should seek to tip the balance away from quantity and back towards quality. Fewer and better patents, which retain their validity in the courts, would in the longer term be the most efficacious way of reducing the burden on the major patent offices and, more importantly, securing widespread support for the patent system.[40]

This last issue continues to represent the most severe Achilles' heel for the global governance of IPRs, but without some generalized legitimacy, enforcing and protecting IPRs in a wider sense remains a difficult if not impossible task. However, the Patent Agenda for many critics seems to be concerned only with the system's legitimacy among its "users," which is to say the corporations that patent most widely, rather than any other interested parties.

Reflecting the Patent Agenda's "quantity" focus, since the turn of the millennium two significant sets of patent treaty negotiations have taken place at the WIPO under the agenda's auspices: the Patent Law Treaty (PLT) defines a single set of rules for preparing, filing and managing patents in signatory countries; and the Substantive Patent Law Treaty (SPLT), that has yet to be finalized but is intended to encompass rules regarding the scope or subject matter of patents, exclusions and rules for deciding between competing claims. Moreover, alongside these negotiations, the shifts they have produced as regards patentability, for instance, are already feeding into the revision of the PCT, through consideration of issues that the PLT raises by the working group examining how the PCT might be amended.[41] Although the prospect of reforming the PCT has been quite widely welcomed, by many developing countries as well as the developed countries, the difficulty of reaching agreement on reforms, such as including third party interests as a way of guarding against illegitimate or unfounded patent applications, has continued to limit any final proposals.

The reform of the PCT is intimately tied to the new Patent Law Treaty, the most important aspect of which is the relaxation of requirements for the submission of patent applications, allowing early and partial submission of applications, as well as shifting the burden of proof as regards fraud or procedural shortcomings to the complaining party.[42] These new practices are intended to raise the throughput of patent applications and grants, by reducing the procedures that applications must go through, and are clearly parallel to the attempts to reform the PCT as regards the standards and criteria of patenting. However, deploying the Commission's distinction, it seems unlikely that the relaxation of procedures at the heart of the PLT will do much to *raise* the quality of patents that are handled through the PCT processes; indeed, it is more likely to expand the number of problematic and contentious patents.

If an agreement can be reached, and it is by no means certain that an agreement *can* be reached, the key elements that are to be harmonized by the SPLT are: the establishment of patentability, to limit or remove national interpretations of the criteria for recognizing a qualifying invention; the determination of the characteristics of an "invention" for the purpose of patenting, to remove the "technical" aspect, expanding the scope of patents to include, for instance, "business methods," software and "research tools" such as Expressed Sequence Tags in genomics; and the scope of patent protection, to reduce the possibility of using environmental or public health criteria for limiting grants otherwise covered by patent criteria. This goes well beyond the TRIPs agreement and as such seeks to remove national determination of these issues. The SPLT would also aim to harmonize the "doctrine of equivalents" that governs what is regarded as an infringement, that is, how close similarities are before they are regarded as equivalent to the patented technology. More importantly, the SPLT includes a provision to prohibit contracting parties from establishing any further conditions for patenting apart from those explicitly laid out in the treaty.[43] The SPLT therefore is essentially intended to raise the "floor" set by the TRIPs agreement.

Perhaps more surprisingly, the SPLT also seeks to harmonize the definition of "prior art" within patent examination and by doing so may again remove considerable national flexibilities. However, if the definition of prior art is widened, then Biswajit Dhar and R.V. Anuradha have argued,

> the emphasis in the draft regulations to the SPLT that information made public by whatever means, including oral communication,

could actually prove beneficial to a country like India, where traditional knowledge associated with much of [their] biological
resources exists in oral form. If such oral knowledge was considered by the patent offices in every country for determining prior
art, it could reduce the instances of frivolous patents.[44]

Whether this provision will survive the negotiation process remains to
be seen. The more extensive the prior art that will be recognized, the
more difficult it is to demonstrate "newness" for patents, and thus it
seems likely that such a wide definition might well be reined in
during continued negotiations at the WIPO, as it is unlikely to receive
the support of corporate "advisors" to national negotiating teams.

The political project behind the draft agreement is to remove the
remaining flexibility that, although difficult to operationalize, has so
far remained within the TRIPs mandated system of governance. Indeed,
the SPLT is intended to set a clear limit on any further limitations that
national legislatures might regard as a political response to local problems and issues. If the SPLT is to be ratified at the WIPO, for those
states that signed on, their governments' ability to shape their patent
law to their specific circumstances will be further circumscribed. If it
gets to this stage significant bilateral pressure will surely be applied to
ensure accession. These changes are required if the "universal" global
patent is to become a reality, and would make the balance between
public and private benefits, at the center of the law of IPRs since their
original legislative emergence, a global matter. However, there are few,
if any, mechanisms that allow the social or public interest to be fully
articulated at this global level, as I will discuss in the final chapter.

Conversely, the evident difficulty of finalizing a text of the SPLT
itself may indicate that the high-water mark for the global governance
of IPRs has been reached, despite the efforts of the WIPO to further
extend its scope; without further normative (re)construction, it is
unlikely that the SPLT will become international law. This is not
because the developed countries recognize the problems other members
of the WIPO might encounter in signing on to the SPLT, but rather
because the remaining differences between the US, the EU and Japan
are much more difficult to resolve and are much less susceptible to
bilateral political pressure.[45] While TRIPs harmonized those aspects of
the IPR system that were already essentially the same across the
leading "trilateral" countries, the SPLT requires that these major
players also have to compromise in areas of their national practice,
making agreement that much harder to reach now that they may need
to compromise *their* autonomy. However, despite these difficulties the

private sector is pushing the SPLT as part of a long-term project of widening patent harmonization.

This conflict of interests between the major industrialized states, the developing countries and the private sector reveals the wider difficulties of global governance of which the WIPO is exemplary. As noted at the beginning of this chapter, the notion of global governance tries to capture the possibility of political leadership that major international organizations and other actors can potentially develop. However, given the continuing salience of state sovereignty this potential is hardly unlimited, and may be compromised when the strategic direction favored by the governing organization conflicts with perceived national interests. With markets increasingly the subject of governance at the supra-national, or multilateral level, the private sector also has significant interests that are well articulated through various lobbying groups as well as through national delegations in any specific set of negotiations. The difficulties that the WIPO has confronted in the discussions of the SPLT reveal very clearly the four corners of the "problem" of contemporary global governance.

Not only are the interests of the developed countries and the (broadly defined) developing countries unlikely to be easily aligned through negotiation, the strategic plans of the organization itself, as well as the interests of the private sector also have to be co-ordinated if there is to be significant institutional innovation; in this case if the SPLT is to be signed and subsequently ratified. At lower levels of harmonization and globalization of governance, agreement has been fostered by aligning the interests of three of these groups: the WIPO itself, the private sector and the developed countries, while also offering minimal compromises and "horse trading" at the WTO to keep the majority of developing countries on board. However, now that differences have emerged in one of the key groups, with national interest in flexibility again being asserted, as it was throughout much of the history of the WIPO, reaching a similar level of consensus as that which allowed the "ratcheting up" of the global governance at the end of the last millennium may not be possible.

Apart from these formalized instruments that are intended to further expand the protection available for IPRs across the global system, the WIPO has therefore also attempted to adopt a "soft law" approach for other forms of IPRs, through programs of registration and arbitration, as well as through its program of technical assistance. However, in launching the Patent Agenda and seeking to further consolidate the protection of IPRs at the global level, the WIPO has also engendered a relatively well-organized reaction among its developing country members and interested non-governmental organizations. Recently there has been a concerted campaign in Geneva among the developing country representatives at the WIPO, supported by a number of focussed NGOs, to establish a Development Agenda for the WIPO. This has centered on the role of the WIPO as a specialized agency of the United Nations, and a number of critics have argued that the WIPO, despite its formal links as a United Nations specialized agency, has not operated in line with the developmental concerns of the UN system. This and other problems that beset the WIPO are the subject of the next chapter.

5 The "Problem" with the WIPO

So far we have examined the World Intellectual Property Organization's history and organizational structure, as well as aspects of its role in the global governance of intellectual property rights (IPRs). Already it has become apparent that the WIPO's activities are hardly unproblematic, and indeed for many it is the WIPO itself that is in need of reform, or at least a change in political orientation. Peter Drahos has argued that one of the key problems that besets the WIPO, especially given its regained place in international IPR-related policy making, is that most developing countries send representatives from their intellectual property offices to its meetings.[1] Certainly these individuals may have good technical knowledge, itself often derived from the WIPO's many training schemes, but they have little interest in, or knowledge of, the public policy aspects of IPRs as regards regulation or economic development. In other words, and possibly quite purposefully, they have been inculcated into the technical view of intellectual property.

Therefore, while the Africa Group has been quite effective in the TRIPs Council at the World Trade Organization (WTO), there has until recently been no equivalent counterpart among developing country representatives, from sub-Saharan Africa or elsewhere, at the WIPO.[2] The WIPO's characterization of itself as a technical organization has paid a dividend for those developed countries that have wanted to focus on pushing the harmonization agenda forward, raising standards of protection and enforcement. Until the turn of the new millennium *political* issues were effectively kept out of the WIPO's deliberations; most discussions have merely been about the refinement of the relevant international treaties, and establishment of better cross-border enforcement of rights. Indeed, technical assistance, as a socialization mechanism "educating" patent office personnel, trade negotiators and policy makers across the developing countries, not only produces advocates for IPRs, but also encourages their acceptance of the WIPO Patent Agenda when they are negotiating on behalf of their governments in Geneva.

The shaping of the agenda that takes place during meetings and training at the WIPO has already had a significant effect on the shape of policies "voluntarily" adopted across many developing countries.[3] Utilizing "soft law" methods, as well as training and technical assistance, the WIPO's international bureau has demonstrated a clear understanding of the centrality of norms in the politics of establishing IPR-related legislation. Indeed, in his history of the first twenty-five years of the organization, Arpad Bogsch asserted that one of its central

> tasks is the establishment of norms that oblige the Member States to grant a certain level of protection to the creators and owners of intellectual property, particularly where they are foreigners. That is why we speak of international protection and that is why a world organization and international treaties are needed. The norms require constant revision because the social, cultural, technical and economic conditions of mankind are constantly evolving and the institutions of our civilization – including the institution of intellectual property – must evolve with them to remain useful. It is the World Intellectual Property Organization that is responsible for keeping the institution of intellectual property useful in such changing circumstances.[4]

Thus, the notion that the WIPO is an organization centrally concerned with socialization is not merely an analysis made by critics, but rather was seen by its long-serving Director General as a key element in the organization's mission and activities.

While the current Director General, Kamal Idris, sees this program of socialization as one of "demystification,"[5] Edward Kwakwa, at the time an assistant legal counsel at the WIPO, suggested in 2002 that the "challenge is how to make [the] WIPO and an intellectual property normative framework more effective and relevant in an attempt to increase universal compliance with fundamental intellectual property norms, while maintaining selectivity in the production of new standards."[6] Thus, the focus on norms continues to be central to the WIPO's focus even where other issues enter the staff's considerations.

However, this well-developed program of socialization has now begun to meet some resistance, perhaps most obviously in the proposals to establish a Development Agenda at the WIPO to complement the WIPO's own Patent Agenda. In the next section I discuss this proposal, before moving to the key issue that this raises: the relationship between the WIPO and the United Nations. If the WIPO is to benefit from being a specialized agency of the UN, then a number of critics have begun to argue that this link must be made to mean something more than a mere formal link; the WIPO must more explicitly adopt the overall developmental priorities of the UN system. This then leads me to look more widely at the question of how neutral or technical the WIPO might actually be, before setting these issues in the wider context of the overall realm of global governance.

The WIPO Development Agenda: Mainstreaming Development at the World Intellectual Property Organization

At the beginning of September 2004, Argentina and Brazil informally circulated to the members of the WIPO a proposal to be discussed in the then imminent General Assembly; this would become the proposal to establish a Development Agenda for the WIPO.[7] Although there had been some discussion of the developmental dimension of intellectual property at previous General Assemblies, this was the first time since the WIPO's establishment that a formal agenda had been proposed, rather than merely a fragmented set of measures raised during Assembly meetings. This more formal proposal reflected a number of NGO-facilitated seminars and research reports, including the influential report from the UK Commission on Intellectual Property Rights,[8] and its linked workshops and final conference, where the position articulated in the Development Agenda itself had started to be explored. Almost immediately the proposal gathered another eleven developing country co-sponsors (Bolivia, Cuba, Dominican Republic, Ecuador, Egypt, Iran, Kenya, Sierra Leone, South Africa, Tanzania and Venezuela) and became the focus for developing country negotiations at the WIPO, led by the "Group of Friends of Development."

The proposed Development Agenda focuses on the assertion that has been central to the WIPO's practices; that the WIPO exists to "promote intellectual property." The proposal calls into question the compatibility of this goal with the expected objectives of an agency associated with the UN. During the October 2004 WIPO General Assembly it was unanimously agreed that this therefore meant that intellectual property could only be "promoted" to the extent that such promotion also served the developmental aims of the wider UN system.[9] Furthermore, as the Brazilian representative noted, the proposal also represented the views of a wide range of academics and non-governmental organizations that had recently signed the Geneva Declaration on the Future of the WIPO, likewise arguing for a more clearly defined set of developmental priorities for the organization.[10] However, while the developing country sponsors of the Development Agenda saw this as a wide-ranging set of issues that should help (re)shape the WIPO's overall approach to the question of intellectual property, perhaps unsurprisingly, many of the developed country representatives at the Assembly, while willing to acknowledge the role of IPRs in development, also wished to limit the scope of discussion to the question of technical assistance.

The WIPO Development Agenda itself starts by quoting a paragraph from the Doha Development Agenda that was launched during the WTO's fourth Ministerial Conference (in November 2001). This acts to link the WIPO Development Agenda to the Doha deliberations, and to a wider range of proposals and actions that have "all placed development at the heart of their concerns."[11] This initial statement was then followed by seven agenda items:

1   The "development dimension" has been increasingly recognized across the institutions of global governance, and through the Doha Development Agenda has specifically been introduced into the realm of the global governance of IPRs;

2   As the WIPO is a specialized agency of the UN it is already mandated to "take into account the broader development goals that the UN has set for itself, in particular the Millennium Development Goals" and this should be reflected more clearly in the perspectives and practices of the WIPO itself;

3   Recognizing the crucial norm-setting activities of the WIPO, as related to the negotiations towards the Substantive Patent Law Treaty, for instance, the WIPO must recognize and include not merely the need for national flexibilities in supporting developmental aims, but must also better recognize the public-regarding dimension of intellectual property;

4   Because technological transfer is a key element to development, and because, despite claims to the contrary, the international IPR-system has not fostered extensive transfers of technology, a new subsidiary body of the WIPO needs to be established to look at what measures could be taken to reduce the barriers to transfer of both technology and scientific research;

5   One of the key areas that has concerned developing countries has been enforcement, and thus the Advisory Committee on Enforcement, set up by the WIPO in 2002, "should be guided by

a balanced approach to intellectual property enforcement" and not merely focus on the interests of rights' holders and curbing infringement. Rather, equity and the issue of anti-competitive practices must be included in the committee's work;

6   Technical assistance needs to be better tailored to individual countries' needs and also needs to be more focussed on balancing the costs and benefits of protecting intellectual property; such support must also focus on how developing countries can maximize the benefits of the existing flexibilities in the Trade Related Aspects of Intellectual Property Rights (TRIPs) agreement;

7   The WIPO itself must serve all sectors of society, as well as the interests of all its members. Too often the WIPO has conflated user-groups and other NGOs, and thus has not fully recognized the public-regarding dimension of the protection of IPRs, but rather has emphasized the interests of private and commercial rightsholders.

As will be immediately apparent a number of the issues raised by the WIPO Development Agenda have already been noted in the discussion of the organization in previous chapters.

During the General Assembly's initial discussions the representative of the US asserted that the Development Agenda "appeared to be premised on the misconception that strong intellectual property protection might be detrimental to global development goals and that the WIPO had disregarded development concerns", and stressed that the "thought that weakening intellectual property would further development was as flawed as the idea that an intellectual property system alone could bring about development."[12] However, this largely misrepresented the proposal; it sought neither to generally reduce the protection for IPRs, nor to suggest that intellectual property was the only problem. Rather the Development Agenda seeks a re-orientation of the WIPO towards a more developmental set of concerns, and sets out the argument that the protection and enforcement of IPRs cannot be seen as an end in itself.

These sorts of misunderstandings led the Group of Friends of Development to refine and further develop the proposed Development Agenda.[13] This work also prompted a formal proposal from the US Government, suggesting the establishment of a Partnership Program for the WIPO reflecting its existing and sufficient development orientation.[14] The US proposal aimed to rework some of the technical assistance programs already delivered by the WIPO, but argued at some length that a wholesale reorientation of the WIPO is not required as it is already (potentially) able to fulfill the role the Development Agenda envisages for the organization. Indeed, it is apparent that forces similar to those that were able to sideline the Brazilian UN resolution on IPRs from 1961 are moving to attempt to stifle and limit the impact of the WIPO Development Agenda, although this time the political context in which these debates are played out is a little different.[15]

Like the staff of the WIPO's International Bureau, the representatives of the developed countries have recognized that the dispute concerns the normative under-pinning of the governance of intellectual property itself. The key demand of the Development Agenda is to re-establish, at the global level, the traditional public policy aspects of intellectual property, and specifically how public policy ends can be related to IPRs. This goes against the privileging of private rights that has informed most IPR-related global governance since the establishment of the TRIPs agreement.[16] The underlying logic of the Development Agenda, therefore, is perhaps best understood as an attempt to "mainstream development" at the WIPO. Most importantly its supporters stress that contrary to the position adopted by the US delegation, the agenda impacts on all the various elements of the WIPO's activities, including the expansion of differential treatment among the members, directly related to their levels of development. It is here that very clearly the developing and developed country members of the WIPO disagree: mainstreaming development for the Group of Friends of Development, and their supporters, is much more than merely adding new "tools" to the technical assistance program.

Furthermore, the Group has become more strident in arguing that the WIPO must be seen as a membership organization, and as an intergovernmental institution it is intended to serve its state members. The WIPO should not be regarded in any way as dependent on, or subservient to the private rightsholders who use its services. As one of the Group's more recent statements puts it: the WIPO

is answerable to its member states and its existence depends on its Members only. The global protection systems which contribute significantly to WIPO's income are systems that have been created by Member States. Rightholders must not lose sight of the central role played by Member States in the establishment of these services. Consequently, as much as the International Bureau should strive to provide efficient services as mandated by Members, payment for these services by rightholders should in no way provide the basis for anyone to claim that the users of these protection systems have the right to determine the agenda or priorities of the Organization.[17]

However, given that these corporations also have significant leverage with many of the members of the WIPO, it is not clear that this influence can so easily be restrained or limited. Indeed, *Intellectual Property Watch* recently reported that one industry representative claimed that they were in Geneva, for the October 2005 WIPO General Assembly, to follow an "anti-development agenda."[18]

After being first presented to, and welcomed by, the WIPO's General Assembly the Development Agenda was the subject of three Inter-Sessional Intergovernmental Meetings (IIM) in 2005. Once certain technical issues about the capacity of the IIM to discuss reform had been settled, the Agenda prompted a wide range of further proposals during these meetings; these ranged from a number of representations from developed country members of the WIPO and their supporters that suggested there should be either no, or only minimal, reform, to proposals from other members of the WIPO that proposed a more radical reorientation and restructuring of the organization as the only way it could be made to serve the developmental needs of the majority of its members.[19] However, not all developing country members of the WIPO fully support the proposal, with the group that does depicted by some commentators as merely seeking to reduce the input costs for their emergent industries, rather than being interested in development more widely.[20]

The proposals that are most critical of the organization recognize that while the WIPO has performed relatively well as regards service provision (e.g. the Patent Cooperation Treaty) and dispute settlement (e.g. the Uniform Domain Name Dispute Resolution Policy), it has been less successful in serving the interests of its developing country members in its negotiations over new treaties and agreements, has failed to fully establish evidential links between development and intellectual property, and has also failed to appreciate or properly assess the actual impact on countries of the rules it supports and the technical assistance it delivers.[21] However, because many of the developed country members' representatives in Geneva do not accept the criticisms leveled at the WIPO and its practices, there has been little agreement on how to take the agenda forward.

While there has been some discussion of the establishment of a specialized Standing Committee on Intellectual Property and Development, many developing countries' representatives see this as a mechanism by which the WIPO secretariat and the developed countries can effectively (again) sideline developmental concerns.[22] As before, these debates have mostly pitched the developing countries against the developed country members of the WIPO. A number of the developed countries have argued that the scope of the existing Permanent Committee on Cooperation for Development Related to Intellectual Property could be expanded to deal with the developmental issues raised by the Development Agenda. For many of the Agenda's supporters, as this committee failed to expand the developmental dimension at the WIPO in the past, this could be no solution, and after the third IIM, the General Assembly agreed to its abolition, the first shift in procedures prompted by the Development Agenda, albeit a relatively minor victory.[23]

At the center of the Development Agenda debate are differing assessments of the scope and previous success of the WIPO's activities. For the rich developed countries the UN does not need another development agency, and they suggest both the United Nations Development Program (UNDP) and the United Nations Conference of Trade and Development (UNCTAD) are suitable forums for dealing with developmental issues, not the WIPO which should remain a technical agency. Ironically, UNCTAD for many years was very active as regards intellectual property issues, specifically linked to the transfer of technology, but was effectively marginalized during the Uruguay Round of multilateral trade negotiations, and has not recovered its influence on the global governance of intellectual property since.[24]

For the developed countries, the promotion of development issues at the WIPO is essentially a matter of technical assistance to bring countries into compliance with their TRIPs-related commitments, from which the developmental benefits will then flow by definition. This limited view of the scope of the WIPO's activities is contested by the developing countries' representatives: firstly on the grounds that actually the WIPO is already more a norm-generating organization than merely a supplier of technical support; and secondly, the WIPO must integrate developmental concerns into its workings because the use and extension of IPRs actually has considerable, and often detrimental effects on developing countries' developmental paths.

This division has also been reflected in the views of a number of interested non-state parties. Thus, civil society organizations have mostly lined up on the side of the Friends of Development, while industry organizations have supported the position against reform adopted by the US, the EU and other developed countries' representatives.[25] However, while the debates around the Brazilian UN resolution some forty years ago were notable for the major involvement of private commercial non-state parties, in the recent debates non-governmental groups have also been actively involved, supporting the developing countries both politically and with well-developed research.[26] There has also been some divergence between the developed countries' positions, with the EU (under the leadership of the UK in the second half of 2005) seeking to extend the discussions while also "harvesting" those proposals from the agenda that already have wider support.[27] Even so, the most widely supported proposals are those linked to technical assistance, and therefore the Development Agenda's wider concerns and dynamic remain at present frustrated by resistance from the WIPO's most powerful members.

While clearly the proposals that form the Development Agenda are still being discussed, it seems unlikely that there will be any immediate change at the WIPO. The Provisional Committee that has been empowered to examine the issues around the WIPO Development Agenda is an unprecedented form of deliberation at the WIPO and thus its ability to fulfill its mandate is currently unknown.[28] The danger is that without a formal existence, and despite comments by members of the WIPO staff that it might be considered a "stepping stone" to a permanent committee, the deliberations and conclusions of the Provisional Committee may be relatively easily ignored.[29]

Making the United Nations Link Mean Something

This lack of change in the perspectives and practices of the WIPO becomes more problematic if, as many critics argue, the WIPO is to properly function as a specialized agency of the UN. A major element in the politics behind the Development Agenda has been the argument that the WIPO is not driven by any significant development concerns, but rather by the "logic" of the benefits of establishing IPRs across the global system. This, as Sisule Musungu and Graham Dutfield have pointed out, sits in direct contrast to a wider reading of the WIPO's mandate and purpose based on the agreement that the organization made with the United Nations in 1974. Musungu and Dutfield note that:

> The Agreement clearly states that [the] WIPO's role is subject to the competence and responsibilities of the UN and its organs . . . Therefore, while [the] WIPO has a specialized competence on matters of intellectual property, the intention was clearly that its mandate should be constructed in the context of the development objectives of the specified UN agencies as well as the broader

objectives of achieving international co-operation in solving problems of an economic, social, cultural and humanitarian character, and in promoting and encouraging respect for human rights and fundamental freedoms.[30]

The key point is that for an organization to become, and continue to be a specialized agency of the UN, its purposes must be compatible with those of the other UN agencies and more generally with the UN's political perspective as expressed through the General Assembly. To critics of the WIPO's current practices this suggests that a key element in (re)establishing a public-regarding aspect to global policy making in the realm of IPRs is to hold the WIPO to the undertakings it made when it was originally recognized as a UN specialized agency.

However, setting out exactly what this means in practice is a little more difficult. Those developed country representatives that have dismissed the Development Agenda's central concerns have argued that the WIPO does not have the resources to support wider developmental objectives, and in any case it lacks the expertise in development that would be required to fulfill such demands. Underlying this position is the assumption that economic development is best served by rewarding the innovative and creative work of individuals, and this is best achieved through strong and enforceable intellectual property rights. If this does produce social costs these should be ameliorated through foreign aid and other developmental support, rather than through the procedures and activities of the WIPO itself, which should be reserved for its core mission of "promoting" IPRs. The WIPO deals with technical issues; the political aspects of development can be separated from these issues, and dealt with perfectly satisfactorily elsewhere. However, for those that wish to see the WIPO more closely reflect the UN's developmental concerns, this is much too narrow a reading of the WIPO's mandate and much too simplistic an understanding of the manner in which the international enforcement of IPR affects, or may even constrain the developmental trajectories of many countries.

The agreement between the UN and the WIPO set out how the two organizations would co-ordinate their activities and co-operate over their strategic direction, with article 5 establishing a clear obligation for the WIPO to follow any recommendations of the UN, and work with a number of named agencies, including the UNCTAD, the UNDP and the UN Educational Scientific and Cultural Organization (UNESCO), to develop resources to tackle problems identified by these specialized agencies in consultation with the WIPO. Where developmental problems linked to the enforcement of IPRs were raised by other agencies, the WIPO had a clear obligation to address these questions and suggest solutions to ameliorate the specific problems identified.

Likewise, article 10 of the agreement obliged the WIPO to work with the UNCTAD, the UNDP and the UN Industrial Development Organization (UNIDO) to promote and facilitate the transfer of technology and to thereby support these agencies' specific developmental objectives. Here, issues of non-working of patents and other anticompetitive practices have been at the forefront of the developing countries' concerns since well before the conclusion of the Uruguay Round. Hence, as Musungu and Dutfield have argued, it is not possible for the WIPO to legitimately limit its concerns to the narrower technical concerns of registration, dispute settlement and technical assistance (where this has merely involved the supply and support for the adoption of laws based on developed country models), and remain a specialized agency of the UN.[31]

Despite the developed countries' representatives' claims that there are other agencies better equipped to deal with the link between intellectual property and development, as noted before, the UNCTAD has been effectively marginalized within the WIPO's negotiations, despite being the agency with the most claim to competence in this area, and the one that has been the locus of much debate and policy discussion among developing countries. Furthermore, other UN agencies with significant interests in IPRs, from UNESCO to the UNDP, have also been effectively excluded from the policy deliberations at the WIPO in the last decade. However, as an immediate response to the Development Agenda proposals, the WIPO's secretariat undertook to arrange meetings with a number of agencies of the UN, and other "stakeholders," to discuss the issue of development and intellectual property,[32] a tacit admission that not enough had been undertaken in this regard in the past.

Whether this leads to any reorientation of the WIPO remains to be seen. And even if this does involve some shift in the WIPO's focus and/or mission, it is notable that where the organization has had closer contact with UN agencies, such as in its work with UNESCO on traditional knowledge, it is far from clear that the UN agencies have been able to modify the WIPO's orientation; rather on traditional knowledge, at least, UNESCO seems to have adopted the focus on IPRs as a solution to the problem of non-community exploitation, following the WIPO, not the other way round. In other words, contrary to the hopes of the supporters of the WIPO Development Agenda, the political influence has been in the opposite direction to that desired.

Therefore, while there seems to be a clear argument for linking the work of the WIPO to the wider concerns of the UN, as argued for by the Development Agenda, it is difficult to know how successful this might actually be. The WIPO's International Bureau openly accepts that as a specialized agency of the UN they are required to be cognizant of, and clearly consider, the views of other UN agencies. Thus, it is incumbent on the developing countries working through these linked agencies to introduce the wider developmental dimension into the WIPO's deliberations.[33] These interactions are already clearly mandated by the WIPO's agreement with the UN and therefore may be the avenue through which the concerns of the Development Agenda can be brought into the heart of the WIPO's activities, even if they are resisted elsewhere in the organization's operations. However, as already noted, this also then comes up against the manner in which the global governance of intellectual property has been effectively depoliticized by the assumption that the WIPO is merely a technical agency, and it is to this more general issue that I now turn.

The Question of the World Intellectual Property Organization's Neutrality

Underlying the problems that have prompted the proposals for a WIPO Development Agenda is an argument about whether the WIPO acts neutrally, and serves the interests of all its members equally. As the WIPO's key mission is to promote the use and protection of IPRs, this issue can be divided into two separate questions: first, is the institution of intellectual property itself merely a legal mechanism that has no *political* dimension?; and second, whatever the assumed political character or social role of IPRs, has the WIPO itself taken account of, and acted on, the interests of all its members equally? Although intimately linked, these two questions also suggest quite different domains of inquiry and political engagement.

Briefly, taking the wider question about intellectual property first: given that the institution of intellectual property is premised on a balance between private rights to reward and public benefits of access to and distribution of knowledge goods, products and services, the position that intellectual property is merely a legal and technical mechanism cannot stand. Certainly some defenders of intellectual property have lamented its *politicization* by critics, but this misses its key characteristic: although often defended on the basis of natural rights-linked discourse using the narratives discussed in the first chapter, or on the basis of economic efficiency, intellectual property is a policy intervention aimed to support specific *political* goals, and always has been since patents were first established in fifteenth century Venice.[34] At the center of the protection of intellectual property is a balance that is constantly the subject of political reassessment: the WIPO is establishing a political mechanism that has historically been intended to produce policy-related outcomes. The difficulty is that the political interests of the WIPO's various members are not aligned in any clear manner, and thus, by virtue of the character of intellectual property itself there will always be political disputes about the international distribution of benefits and costs.

While intellectual property was governed and regulated at the national level, these political disputes could be mediated through normal political processes of law, and the articulation of conflicting interests through whatever political processes were available in a national polity. The history of intellectual property has been a long history of dispute between those who favored the widening of the scope, and strengthening of protection, that holders of IPRs might benefit from, and those who, for policy reasons, wanted to ensure that public dissemination of knowledge and information was as wide as practicable. For five hundred years policy makers have sought to establish a balance between the incentive to invent and create through the award of property rights in the results of intellectual activities, and the social dissemination of the results of these activities. Whereas policy makers wanted new information and techniques distributed as widely and as quickly as possible to aid economic and social development, they also wanted to stimulate the activities that produced these intellectual resources. More single-mindedly, rightsholders, often with powerful political allies, have wanted to reap the financial rewards of control for as long as possible, and thus have usually sought to widen the scope and lengthen the term of the rights awarded. These opposed interests led to fraught debates and disputes, as well as shifting legal balances between these interests as manifest in the law of intellectual property across various times and jurisdictions.

Now that the governance of intellectual property has been partly relocated to the global level through the establishment of the TRIPs agreement, while national legislatures still have some contribution to make to these debates, considerations related to the central political balance have been shifted into the global political realm. Although not the only multilateral forum implicated in these debates, the WIPO is a key location for debates and actions regarding the current manifestation of this political problem. Hence, if the first question noted above to a large extent can be answered in the negative, *intellectual property is not merely a technical mechanism*, then the second question regarding the recognition of contending interests by the WIPO becomes the central political issue that confronts the organization, its supporters and critics. If there is nothing neutral about IPRs, then "promoting" them must also be *political*, and thus the WIPO's members' interests are unlikely to be easily coordinated, and indeed this is exactly what the recent politics of the WIPO would indicate.

In the post-TRIPs decade governments of many countries have become worried about the impact of TRIPs compliance on other political priorities, including economic development, technology transfer and public health priorities. Whereas in the past these policy ends could have been co-ordinated with the establishment and regulation of IPRs on the basis of national political bargains, these options are now severely constrained. Moreover, various non-governmental groups, sometimes grouped together as "civil society," have worked hard to publicize the social costs of recognizing strong owners' rights in the realm of knowledge and information, perhaps most successfully as regards pharmaceutical patents and their impact on those living with AIDS in Asia, Latin America and sub-Saharan Africa. Furthermore technological changes, especially digitization, have caused companies in some industrial sectors to become increasingly concerned about the ability of even TRIPs-compliant legislation to protect their business models. Here the music industry is emblematic, with its desire to constrain consumer activity through the introduction of legally protected digital rights management technologies.

Therefore, rather than finally establishing the neutral and technical character of intellectual property, the TRIPs agreement has actually revealed the numerous political problems with recognizing and enforcing IPRs more generally. While some of these debates have been undertaken at the WTO, the TRIPs Council (as part of the WTO) has become deadlocked over different countries' divergent interests in the realm of intellectual property, and how these should be recognized in international trade diplomacy. However, for many critics, this deadlock itself is a useful brake on the further harmonization and expansion of the global governance of intellectual property, even if this lack of progress has also adversely affected the cross-border aspects of the Doha Declaration on the TRIPs Agreement and Public Health relating to the importation of compulsorily licensed medicines by non-producing countries. Conversely, at the WIPO, those arguing for a reassessment of the political balance at the heart of intellectual property had been less successful, until the recent moves around the Development Agenda prompted the reexamination of the WIPO's role in, and impact on, its developing country members.

Commenting on the history of copyright, and its relation to the public interest, Gillian Davies has pointed out that

> it is the law-maker who has the duty to evaluate the issues and the conflicting interests of the various, often warring factions within the interested parties, to consider what justice requires and to take the necessary hard decisions in the general public interest of society as a whole.[35]

A similar conclusion can be drawn more widely to encompass the whole realm of intellectual property, and immediately points to the difficulty that the WIPO is confronted with. On the one hand, the WIPO is concerned with introducing and expanding the protection of IPRs based on already agreed legal standards and mechanisms, but on the other it is also acting to establish further legal agreements.

In the former role, any balancing is meant to be an issue for national legislatures, but the TRIPs agreement, alongside other emerging multilateral instruments, is drafted in such a way as to minimize the flexibility that can be achieved at the national level. This has limited the realm of political deliberation that has in the past accompanied the establishment of IPRs in specific national jurisdictions. Through its technical assistance program the WIPO actually does little to establish practically even the flexibilities that remain. In the latter of these two roles, the deliberation of new instruments at the WIPO has been a process that has been undertaken by a sub-set of the organization's members and hence, the "general public interest of [global] society as a whole" has only been articulated through the ventriloquism of the developed countries' representatives, and the numerous private sector organizations that seek to shape the protection accorded IPRs in the global economy. Here, it is taken as axiomatic that the protection of creators, innovators, and others' IPRs provides social benefits that outweigh any social costs of protection. This has led to a relative lack of consideration of the political economic problems encountered by the developing country members of the WIPO, and the well-documented costs they have encountered.

Given the complex history of IPRs, as James Boyle has pointed out, the "WIPO should be comparatively immune from the fallacy that intellectual property policy should always aim towards stronger rights."[36] However, the organization is in thrall to a "maximalist rights culture" that sees the expansion of IPRs as socially beneficial without consideration for the effects of such protection on non-rights holders except to presume that they automatically benefit from the innovation and creativity supported and stimulated by the award of these rights. That said, the staff of the WIPO may often be more open to the consideration of alternative approaches than its most powerful member countries. Thus Boyle recounts the plight of the proposed meeting at the WIPO on the open source alternatives to proprietary software, which while welcomed by the staff was undermined and eventually cancelled through the actions of the US Patent and Trademark Office which argued such considerations would be contrary to the goals of the WIPO.[37] Thus, to some extent, the "problem" for the WIPO is how to balance the strongly articulated interests of its most powerful members with the interests of its more numerous, but politically weaker, developing country members.

Certainly, one of the reasons that negotiations over the next stage of the global governance of IPRs moved back to the WIPO was this ability to conduct negotiations, and establish treaties among non-comprehensive groupings, and thus sideline those likely to object to a further expansion of the realm of governance for intellectual property. Indeed, the developed countries, primarily the US, the EU and Japan, see the WIPO and the WTO as two parts of a single system that allows them to undertake decision-making and policy-generation where it will be most effective.[38] In this sense, it is very useful that the WIPO is a forum that actually does not finally *require* all its members' interests to be taken into account as regards each individual aspect of negotiations regarding new treaties and agreements. Thus, higher or more robust standards can be developed by a focussed group of WIPO members before being presented to the wider membership, and then to the members of the WTO, as emergent international norms. However, as the WIPO remains formally a membership organization it is difficult for the organization to indefinitely sideline or limit the influence of those members and their representatives that are seeking to establish a divergent set of priorities for the WIPO, if the organization is to remain credible.

A further difficulty is that developing countries' governments frequently do not have the resources, nor often the political will, to fully staff their missions to the WIPO, leading some commentators to suggest that many developing countries have yet to fully appreciate the importance of the WIPO's program of negotiations.[39] Thus, one of the reasons that could be posited for the lack of attention to some developing countries' professed interests is that these countries have failed to fully articulate their interests at the WIPO, and hence it should be unsurprising that the organization represents the interests of the most vocal delegates. Certainly this position might have been defensible up until the recently proposed Development Agenda, but no longer. Rather, as the WIPO has regained its status in the global governance of intellectual property, so it has also opened itself up to the political scrutiny that has already started to focus on the TRIPs agreement and its effects.

Although the WIPO has conducted a major program of normative realignment through its technical assistance and education programs, this has not been sufficient to halt the emergence of critical voices and positions within the delegations to the WIPO itself. Thus, while its institutional bias may be towards the expanded protection of IPRs, this position is no longer shared or tacitly colluded with by many of the WIPO's members. The organization's strategy of putting itself back into the center of the global governance of intellectual property has therefore prompted a relatively unexpected political response, because in the wider context of global governance the usual justifications and legitimations mobilized to support the commodification of knowledge are no longer unexamined nor unchallenged.

Setting the "Problem" in the Wider Context of Global Governance

To set the "problem" of the WIPO in the wider context of the global governance of IPRs we must appreciate the wider global politics of IPRs themselves. Firstly, as Peter Yu reminds us we should not be surprised that the TRIPs agreement may be one-sided in favor of the developed countries, and specifically the US, EU and Japan, because it "is *expected* to be one-sided, given the cross sector bargaining during the negotiating process."[40] This is to say, before we criticize the strategy of the developed countries at the WIPO we must recognize that the acceptance of the TRIPs agreement was part of a complex and wide-ranging series of deals that established the WTO after the Uruguay Round of multilateral trade negotiations. However, as it has turned out, the developing countries' side of these deals has been relatively under-achieved, especially as regards agriculture, and until recently, textiles, while the global governance of IPRs has been on a rising arc ever since.

A key element to the problem is that to a great extent the bargain that resulted from the "horse-trading" during the Uruguay Round has been skewed by the manner in which rights and obligations were set out in the TRIPs' text. The developing countries' obligations to renew their national legislation and the developed countries' rights, as regards their nationals' IPRs, are enforceable through the WTO's dispute settlement mechanism, and are clearly expressed in the text of the TRIPs agreement. However, as Robert Wade points out, for the complementary set of rights and obligations this is less true. The developing countries' right to economic development and the developed countries' obligation to aid technology transfer to underpin that right, are much more difficult to enforce, and indeed have been the subject of considerably less protracted effort by the WIPO, nor are they easily introduced into the dispute settlement mechanism of the WTO. These obligations and rights are only set out in general terms in the TRIPs agreement's text and are much more difficult and expensive to litigate at the global level as they are relatively under-specified.[41] All rights seem to reside with the owners of IPRs, whereas all duties reside with the users.

In one area the developed countries *are* to some extent fulfilling their obligations; most developing countries are likely to be dependent on the WIPO's technical assistance to establish the mechanisms and legal infrastructure required by their TRIPs obligations because such political-legal transformations require considerable resources and investment. But as I have already suggested, these programs mostly represent a process of socialization for WTO members, and as such present the form of IPRs constituted in TRIPs as a technical solution to a set of problems regarding posited "market failure" in knowledge and information utilization. Although this does not self-evidently serve many developing countries' immediate best interests, in an attempt to ensure their clients are not caught up in costly IPR-related trade disputes with developed country members of the WTO, the staff of the WIPO have often encouraged developing countries to adopt legislation that goes beyond the formal requirements of the TRIPs agreement.[42] In any case, and in the wake of bi-lateral trade and/or investment agreements with the US or EU, a number of developing countries have found themselves needing "TRIPs-plus" legislation which again reinforces this dynamic within the WIPO's assistance program. Thus, in trying to help developing countries avoid trade disputes, the WIPO's assistance programs have often undermined the possibilities of critical engagement with the provisions of the TRIPs agreement itself.

The TRIPs agreement has also engendered a political response, especially in those developing countries where significant groups remain skeptical of the appropriateness of the TRIPs model, of which the farmers' rights movement in India is perhaps the best known example. Recent debates have ranged across a number of sectors, sometimes focussing on perceptions of bio-piracy,[43] elsewhere concerned with pharmaceutical products, or software piracy, and the "theft" of traditional knowledge.[44] These debates directly affect the legitimacy of the intellectual property norms that are being "imported" into developing countries through the WIPO's programs. However, as Peter Drahos and John Braithwaite point out, whatever critiques may be mobilized against these norms of propertization, the global regime governing IPRs sets "strong limits on a state's capacity to define territorial property rights in ways that enhance national welfare."[45] It is these welfare effects in developing countries that are the central problem in the global governance of IPRs, but welfare is seldom given the weight in trade law that it is elsewhere in international law, and is seldom given significant weight in the WIPO's considerations.

The question of how the WIPO interacts with the rest of the UN system also finds a wider parallel in the debates about how the WTO is related to the extant body of international law. Certainly, the inter-relations between WTO-law and the rest of international law are more complex than attempts to privilege the WTO's rules might imply. Joost Pauwelyn has argued at some length that the laws that can be applied in WTO dispute panels and in the Appellate Body are not limited to *intra*-WTO law. Rather, by virtue of the WTO's legal regime's place within the complex of international law, "a defendant should be allowed to invoke non-WTO rules as justification for breach of WTO rules, even if the WTO treaty itself does not offer such justification (say, with respect to human rights) . . . [and more importantly] non-WTO rules may actually apply before a WTO panel and overrule WTO rules."[46] The assumption that WTO-law should be privileged is a misconception of the WTO's relation with the general body of international law, rather this is a complex and dynamic relationship; the privileging of other agreements over WTO treaty undertakings cannot be assumed one way or the other.

The consideration of this inter-relationship therefore has some resonance with the WIPO Development Agenda's argument that the wider development related treaty undertakings that result from the WIPO's status as a UN special agency must have some salience to its activities. Here, the need to contextualize the global governance of intellectual property within a wider set of developmental objectives seems both logical and well supported. However, at the same time that the "rights" rhetoric is mobilized to justify IPRs within the TRIPs agreement, the practical organization of international property rights has been effectively depoliticized through the juridical systems of enforcement and appeal. By removing conflicts regarding the protection and enforcement of IPRs from the political/diplomatic realm where wider considerations might be easily introduced, and placing them in the legal realm, the TRIPs agreement reduces international disputes to the question of whether specific legislation is TRIPs-compliant; it depoliticizes subsequent disputes.

This depoliticization is then reflected in the self-presentation of the WIPO's role in the global governance of IPRs. If the TRIPs agreement is perceived as essentially legitimate, then this depoliticization and the WIPO's focus on a narrowly conceived notion of technical assistance allows the governance regime to do its intended work. However, it is far from clear that TRIPs *is* regarded as legitimate across the membership of the WTO and the WIPO. Thus, the attempt by the WTO's Appellate Court to limit the relevance of other international legal commitments to international trade law, and the denial of the key shift in emphasis that fully articulating the WIPO's role as a UN specialized agency would involve can be seen as two sides of the same process of depoliticization.

Quite apart from the legitimacy problems that the effects of the TRIPs agreement have engendered, as Daya Shanker has argued, the agreement's legitimacy is also undermined by the way it has been deployed by the more powerful members of the WTO.[47] Not only were the negotiations themselves fraught with dispute, the decisions of the Appellate Body have shifted the demands on developing countries as regards the manner in which their legislation can achieve TRIPs compliance. For instance, while the Appellate Body has been willing to accept administrative, rather than legislative undertakings regarding patenting practice by the US, this has not been the case for India and Brazil among others whose practices closely match the US in the area of parallel importation.[48] The US and the EU have also deployed bilateral pressure to force developing countries to rework their legislation in the manner that undermines the multilateral legal status of TRIPs, and the Appellate Body. The bilateral use of sanctions to enforce GATT/WTO linked law is illegal unless sanctioned by the Appellate Court, but this has not halted their continued use by the USTR as regards IPRs.[49]

This has prompted the political reaction that has produced the WIPO Development Agenda and the linked demand that the organization make its role as a specialized agency of the UN more central to its operations. While the post-TRIPs global governance of intellectual property has seen the partial transformation of the WIPO's activities, the organization has also been determined to resist its marginalization, and has sought to demonstrate that it has something to offer to the most powerful countries in the nascent global intellectual property system. However, because of its institutional structure and the perceived need to work through the establishment of norms rather than merely the attempted imposition of externally determined rules, the WIPO also represents a site of potentiality for the political and social forces that seek to question and rework the current international legal settlement as regards IPRs.

6 The WIPO's Rise, Fall and Comeback

As I have recounted in this book the story of the World Intellectual Property Organization (WIPO) began with hopes for the universalization of intellectual property, from which the organization emerged into a period of increasing difficulties concluding with the WIPO's effective marginalization during the Uruguay Round of multilateral trade negotiations. In the last decade the WIPO has essentially fought to regain its relevance in global governance, to a large extent succeeding in reaffirming its importance. Other political events have aided the resurgence of the WIPO, but equally we should recognize that the organization's directors and staff have focussed on the task of ensuring the WIPO would not decline in importance, nor become marginalized as some other specialized agencies of the United Nations have become.

Many of those working in the academic discipline of International Political Economy have been developing analyses of the development of the new and still emerging governance arrangements of the contemporary global political economy. However, it is interesting to note that the WIPO's marginalization in a key transformational period, during the Uruguay Round of multilateral trade negotiations, seems to have led to its relative under-recognition in accounts of the development of global governance in the last decade. This book has been intended to reacquaint analysts with an important international organization.

The key problem the WIPO has encountered in this new period of global governance is that despite its character as a membership organization, the proliferation of treaties under its auspices, alongside their variable ratification, led the WIPO to be perceived with some justification as a weak site of governance. Unable to offer any real method of enforcement, unable to move beyond a mosaic of agreements, the WIPO had become dependent on the organization's administration functions and ability to facilitate bi-lateral agreements between members. Although this bi-lateralism seemed to have been surpassed by the TRIPs agreement, it quite quickly became apparent to the US, the EU and other developed countries, that further enhancing and developing the protection and enforcement of intellectual property would be inordinately difficult at the World Trade Organization. Indeed, the quagmire that the TRIPs Council has found itself mired in, alongside other diplomatic interventions at the WTO by developing countries, has enhanced the attraction of the WIPO's opt-in approach to further treaty negotiation; a "coalition of the willing" would more likely lead to the advances that the private sector in the developed countries demanded of their governments.

These circumstances have allowed the WIPO to regain some measure of its previous influence and importance in the global governance of IPRs, and to a large extent the organization has recovered from the threat of marginalization. In this last chapter I briefly explore the question of the proliferation of forums that the WIPO has benefited from in the post-TRIPs decade. I then reflect on the mobilization of specific political interests at the WIPO and suggest that the organization must be viewed not merely as a provider of technical resources and training, but rather, and linked to the explicit statements by its Director Generals, as an organization that is seeking to shift and transform the normative political economy of intellectual property. This leads me to conclude by placing the questions raised by the continuing influence and activities of the WIPO in the wider political economic context of global governance.

Forum Proliferation in the Global Governance of Intellectual Property

In the relatively common depictions of the global governance of intellectual property rights (IPRs) in the wake of the Uruguay Round, the political processes of negotiation have often been presented as "forum shopping." We are told that powerful states' governments have shifted the forum for policy deliberation to those arenas where their interests can be supported by the mobilization of their abundant political resources. The shift to the WTO represented the advantage that these states' trade negotiators believed that they could secure by offering cross-sectoral deals; by linking the opening of domestic markets to the international trade in agricultural products, with the recognition and enforcement of IPRs, for instance. Likewise, the move back to the WIPO since the turn of the millennium has also been depicted as a case of forum shopping on the basis that the sorts of policy development that will further expand the global regulation of intellectual property can only be achieved through small groups establishing emergent norms that can then be spread before more widespread adoption and eventual introduction into multilateral governance mechanisms.[1]

However, and conversely, this forum shifting might be better seen as a form of "forum proliferation" not least of all because, as Peter Yu has pointed out: "through incorporation by reference, the laws made in one forum increasingly influence the laws made in another forum. For example, panelists from the WTO Dispute Settlement Body increasingly look to WIPO treaties or other forums to resolve the ambiguities in the TRIPs Agreement."[2] Thus, the very flexibilities that are introduced through the ambiguities in the TRIPs agreement, flexibilities that represented the residual negotiating strength of developing countries' representatives in the Uruguay Round, can be undermined, or side-stepped by appealing to the normative settlement established by the WIPO. In line with both organizations' self-perception, as well as the actual terms of their inter-agency agreement, the WTO and the WIPO work together both to expand and promote the international protection of IPRs, while also serving to provide an interactive dual forum for policy deliberation and development.

This forum proliferation introduces both risks and opportunities into the global governance of intellectual property.[3] Certainly there are opportunities for developing countries to develop authoritative proposals as regards specific elements of the "problem" of intellectual property. The most obvious example is the ability under the Convention on Bio-Diversity to produce different legislative settlements as regards the recognition of specific forms of IPRs for bio-genetic resources. Likewise, arguments and debates regarding public health have very clearly fed back into more formalized considerations of the impact of patenting on the provision of medicines in public health emergencies, and here the HIV/AIDs pandemic has become a totemic issue. There have also been extensive discussions in the realm of agriculture-related protection, linked to the protection of farmers' rights to share and re-use seeds, as well as debates about the interaction between human rights and IPRs. In all these areas, the development of well-founded and widely supported political solutions at variance with the overarching normative structure that has been propounded by the TRIPs agreement allows for the possibility for modification and amendment of the regulatory mechanisms at the heart of the global governance of intellectual property.

Conversely, there is also a significant risk. By diluting and fragmenting the political response to regulatory change, by shifting away from the forum that initially established the key elements of the

"TRIPs mindset", which has been instrumental in working through the normative commitments traditionally supported by the WIPO, this forum proliferation may rob the developing countries of the focussed political resources they badly need to balance the political will of the developed countries. Therefore, although there is a clear possibility that the utilization of other forums may allow marginalized interests an ability to develop, and find support for, alternative solutions to the "problem" of intellectual property, it may also ensure that the developed countries that are most influential at the WIPO will retain their influence over the normative development of the global governance of IPRs.

The proliferation of forums means that the WIPO has been unable to rely passively on its expertise or experience to retain its place at the heart of the global governance of IPRs. Therefore, firstly the organization has had to fight hard to (re)establish its relevance, a campaign that has been largely successful, but secondly, and perhaps more importantly, this also suggests that this regained importance is precarious. If the organization continues to provide broadly the sorts of support that its most powerful developed country members demand on behalf of their own IPR-utilizing sectors, then its continued diplomatic importance can be assured. However as a membership organization, the difficulty with this approach is that it may not always be in line with the interests of other members, nor reflect their representatives' perception of what is required in this particular realm of global governance. Although the international secretariat of the WIPO would, I am sure, like to deny the claim, the WIPO is a highly politicized organization, and cannot be regarded merely as an agency providing technical services, as the debates around the WIPO Development Agenda have clearly revealed.

The Deployment of Political Economic Interest

If the WIPO is a political organization, then we should not be surprised that its political economy reflects the wider political economic power disparities that pattern the global system. These disparities both between the developed and developing countries (widely defined) and within the latter, larger group have prompted the debate about the possibility of establishing a Development Agenda at the WIPO to match and balance the organization's existing Patent Agenda. This has been compounded by the varying interests that are articulated even between different ministries in national delegations. It is not always the case that developing countries' representatives foreground developmental issues; partly due to their socialization through the WIPO's programs, and partly as they are sometimes trade negotiators in any case, the developing countries' negotiators often do not emphasize development as much as many non-governmental organizations believe they should. This has led the Quaker United Nations Office (QUNO) to organize workshops and seminars intended to raise awareness among trade ministries and their negotiators of the development aspects of the regulation and recognition of IPRs.

While a number of international NGOs have started to focus on the WIPO more clearly in the past decade, and as such have not only gained observer status at the organization but have started to produce briefing materials for under-resourced delegations,[4] this activity has not matched the political mobilization of international cooperate interests. Equally, many staff at, and contractors with, the WIPO have a self-perception of the organization's essential technical status, while professional legal groups and lawyers have always wielded a considerable amount of influence at the organization. Indeed, Sisule Musungu and Graham Dutfield regard the influence of industry *and* lawyers as "disproportionate" given the actual character of the WIPO.[5] Although civil society groups are becoming more vocal and more engaged with the WIPO, Musungu and Dutfield contend that this has yet to approach a balancing role to the influence wielded by the aggregated corporate interest both within the organization and through national delegations. It remains the case that both developed countries and many developing country members of the WIPO are subject to significant corporate influence at home and in other forums as well. Thus, corporations and their representatives are very effective national lobbyists, and may well manipulate the make-up of delegations to the WIPO, shaping the arguments and debates before they are initiated in Geneva.

In many developing countries specific sectors have started to recognize their own corporate interests in the protection of IPRs; local music industries are the most obvious example. This has meant that developing countries' negotiators often find that they no longer represent a single defined position on national interests regarding IPRs. Nevertheless, the proposal for a WIPO Development Agenda has still managed to garner significant support from developing country members of the WIPO, although this support is by no means comprehensive. Therefore, it is not clear whether the WIPO would be able to fully embrace a Development Agenda even if its most powerful members could be convinced to support this project. Moreover, despite the very clear statement made by the Group of Friends of Development regarding the lack of leverage that fee-paying corporations should have, the WIPO remains ultimately constrained by its dependence on users of the Patent Cooperation Treaty for the bulk of its funding.

About 85 percent of WIPO's income comes from user fees for its services in administering its various treaties.[6] The majority of these users are the globally active corporations that drove the TRIPs agenda and seek to promote expanded IPRs. It is hard to imagine that they will sit by idly as the WIPO takes steps directly against their stated interests. Further, given the fact that WIPO has worked hard to reassert its importance to the Organization for Economic Cooperation and Development (OECD), it seems unlikely that it would be keen to jeopardize this work by directly challenging the expansionist dynamic in intellectual property that is embedded within the rhetoric of a globalized economic system for the new millennium, where the content industries and other users of digitized resources have become the perceived leading sectors in further economic advances.

Therefore, as we might find in the discussions about the utilization of IPRs to protect, or conversely allow the exploitation of traditional knowledge,[7] the WIPO is undoubtedly promoting IPRs as the solution to the problems that many indigenous communities seem to face. If traditional goods and content are exploited by outside commercial organizations without payments to the originating communities then there would seem to be a clear argument for arranging a mechanism that at the very least ensures these communities gain some recompense. However, the difficulties here relate to the identification of an original "owner" for the purposes of contracting, and also the violence to traditional social structures that the individualization of property rights might bring about. In many ways the rendering of traditional knowledge as intellectual property reflects the corporate need to establish clear lines of ownership and reduce the risks of unenforceable contracts with suppliers of creative outputs, rather than any recognition of the rights of indigenous creators and innovators.

This can, of course, be linked to a wider issue of bringing outlying communities into the capitalist property system.[8] Indeed, sometimes it seems that intellectual property is a solution looking for a problem. To take two examples from a recent series of World Bank studies: the World Bank's African Music Project conceives of the problems for African musicians as essentially those that have started to transform the western industry, and therefore offers IPRs as the most appropriate solution. Likewise, the question of indigenous craft designs has been discussed at the World Bank almost entirely through the logic of property and counterfeit, and thus it is no surprise that again the western logic of IPRs is the solution.[9] If a problem is set up as involving "theft" then protecting property rights is always likely to be the "answer": as the saying goes – "when you have a hammer all problems look like nails." This is how specific political economic interests are remaking the domain of intellectual endeavor: by offering a specific solution, whatever the possible problems seem to be, the shift to commodified knowledge and information continues apace.

Political influence at the WIPO is therefore evident in a number of dimensions. Most obviously through the recognition of corporate interests both by the organization itself and by the various national delegations, various industrial sectors have been able to shape the global governance of intellectual property to reflect their interest. To some extent this has been balanced by the work of various civil society organizations that have aimed to provide a different perspective to the dominant view, and have provided support to under-resourced delegations to facilitate the better representation of their national interests. However, the utilization of the services of various major patent offices in the developed countries, and the organization's pool of intellectual property experts, has meant that both explicitly through the shaping of training, but also through those chosen to deliver the various aspects of these capacity building and technical assistance programs, a specific view of the role of IPRs in modern societies is being supported and broadcast. The WIPO's role as an agent of socialization is perhaps its greatest claim to be a central element of global governance. However, it is exactly this role that prompts much of the criticism of the organization.

Cosmopolitan Governance in a "Thin Community"

As Peter Gerhart has pointed out, although the WTO and the WIPO "promote an efficient system of global trade and investment, we [sic] have found no way to tax those who benefit from the efficiency of the global system in order to support those who do not."[10] This question of balancing the private rewards and public costs of protecting intellectual property has long been a contested issue for the legal institutionalization of IPRs. However, the "one-size-fits-all" global legal settlement instituted by the TRIPs agreement and promoted by the WIPO has revealed the central problem for the globalization of IPRs. Its effects already suggest that without well-developed global societal mechanisms able to mediate between private rewards and social goods/public benefits, the notion of a global regime for IPRs is currently difficult, if not impossible to justify.

The global governance of IPRs closely reflects the depiction of the contemporary global polity suggested by Richard Higgot and Morten Ougaard. While there is a "thick interconnectedness" between "political structures, agents and process, with transnational properties," these are as yet only linked by a "thin community that transcends the territorial state."[11] The global polity has yet to replace the sovereign national polity in the realm of political economic governance, but without the replication of the, by no means universal, democratic elements of state rule at the global level, any global polity will remain only a thin community, unable to fully articulate global community interests. Therefore without state-like mechanisms at the supra-national level, any global polity remains unable to fully enact the social controls that have historically been secured through democratic accountability and legislative modification. There remains no developed mechanism through which community empathy can be translated into globalized political action *inside* the structures of global governance, although significant political mobilization takes place outside.

The negotiation and establishment of the TRIPs agreement, and the resurgent importance of the WIPO, alongside the international industry-based, "insider" lobbying groups involved in establishing and expanding the agenda of governance for intellectual property, all fit with the notion of "thick interconnectedness." Not only via the Internet, which itself is very unevenly globalized, but also through the use of new patented technologies and the increasingly globalized reach of brands, the *globalized* interconnectivity of the political economy of knowledge commodification becomes more pronounced by the day. However, there remains only a "thin community" as regards the socio-political justification of IPRs on which the TRIPs agreement is founded. Mechanisms like those previously encoded in domestic law to recognize the social values of and social costs to this community of the enforcement of IPRs are largely absent. The nascent global polity is still treated as an external element; NGOs and others may be placated but they are seldom treated as legitimate political actors representing the community of interest as regards IPRs. This dynamic is being challenged at the WIPO, but the difficulty of mounting this challenge is also being clearly revealed through the contested politics of the proposed Development Agenda.

This difficulty suggests that at present the world is not sufficiently globalized, whatever commentators celebrating the "borderless world" claim, for any political and legal settlement to closely follow previous *national* political bargains; the justifications that have previously been used to underpin IPRs do not have sufficient purchase on the current global situation without a mechanism for recognizing the social costs or downside of any "bargain" which promotes private rewards. As Graeme Dinwoodie stresses:

> the incorporation of intellectual property agreements within trade mechanisms might (if trade concerns become paramount) deprive intellectual property policymaking of the rich palette of *human values* that historically has influenced its formulation. Considering only the ability to exploit comparative advantage in the ownership of intellectual property rights would appear to make international intellectual property policy less multi-dimensional.[12]

It is this lack of multidimensionality that is the key problem: given the vast inequalities evident in the world, the impact of these inequalities is not recognized when the social costs that are required for the continued support of private rewards remain largely hidden in multilateral policy discussions. And while the Development Agenda goes some way to potentially rectifying this shortcoming, equally the developed countries' representatives' attempts to divert or water down the proposed shifts in the WIPO's practices reveal the political problem at the heart of the WIPO.

The current settlement for IPRs may work well for the developed countries, but for developing countries the central bargain at the center of IPRs makes little sense. However, it is exactly this current settlement that the WIPO is seeking to expand and consolidate, despite the fact that for many the private rights of IPR "owners" in the richer states are being purchased at too great a social cost in the developing world. Before TRIPs this imbalance was reflected in the de facto acceptance by developed countries' governments of widespread non-recognition of their nationals' intellectual property by developing countries in the system overseen by the WIPO and its predecessor organization. This was by no means a perfect solution, and a return to the essentially ungoverned character of the pre-TRIPs world of intellectual property is improbable given the increasing acceptance of the "rule of law," nor would such retreat from governance necessarily be advantageous to developing countries themselves. However, the current settlement does not command significant support outside the developed world, and efforts at norm (re)production are already coming up against the very real problems that TRIPs compliance produces in many developing countries.

These problems are clearly reflected in the global political economy of the WIPO. Recognizing the question of normative reproduction, the organization has deployed significant resources to attempt to socialize policy makers, legislators, negotiators and enforcement personnel into the "world of intellectual property." The WIPO encourages them to accept the stories deployed to justify the use of IPRs where the evidence that intellectual property directly promotes innovation and economic development is often absent. As Pamela Samuelson once put it:

> The modern faith in intellectual property does not seem likely to be shaken soon, primarily because the faith is supported by such evidence as high levels of innovation, high levels of investment in innovation and the concomitant prosperity. The intellectual property laws may not have been responsible, but most observers *believe* that these laws played a part.[13]

The WIPO's technical assistance program and its other promotional activities have led some critics therefore to claim that the WIPO is a "faith based" organization that seeks to convert those non-believers it comes into contact with; an evangelical mission for IPRs. The continuing lack of conclusive evidence of a direct *causal* link between IPRs and economic development leaves the WIPO only with a belief based on coincidence, a position that is hardly unassailable.

Some of the members of the WIPO have recognized that there are clear developmental issues that need to be (re)introduced into the debates around the international protection of IPRs. Many of these issues have already been raised in WTO-linked forums, although such debates have meant that the TRIPs Council has been effectively logjammed for some time; concluding a comprehensive agreement on how the global governance of IPRs might better reflect different levels of, and speeds of, development across the membership of the WTO seems currently impossible. The advantage for developed country members of the WIPO, in continuing policy deliberation there rather than at the WTO, is that they can take the process forward even if significant resistance is articulated within the organization itself. But, equally for the supporters of the Development Agenda, their interests can *also* be moved forward while some members of the WIPO continue to argue that development should be kept out of the organization's central remit.

Therefore we can conclude that the WIPO has benefited from forum proliferation, and has fought hard to retain its position at the center of the global governance of intellectual property. However, this is seldom fully recognized in the IPE literature seeking to understand the processes of global governance in the sector or more generally. This small book has been an attempt to ensure that such myopia does not continue; in this it is an explicit argument against the WIPO's own public position that it is merely a technical organization. Certainly, this claim is no longer as widely accepted as it once was, but in the realm of academic analysis it still lingers. I trust that the readers of this book will no longer be so ambivalent about the role of the WIPO in the global governance of intellectual property.

Appendices

Appendix A.1

Music Industry Piracy Statistics

(from: IFPI Recording Industry 2005, Commercial Piracy Report)

Domestic Music Piracy Levels in 2004

Country	Over 50%	25-50%	10-24%	Less than 10%
North America				Canada, USA
Europe	Bulgaria	Croatia	Belgium	Austria
	Czech Republic	Cyprus	Finland	Denmark
	Estonia	Hungary	Netherlands	France
	Greece	Italy	Slovenia	Germany
	Latvia	Poland	Spain	Iceland
	Lithuania	Portugal		Ireland
	Romania	Slovakia		Norway
	Russia			Sweden
	Serbia/Montenegro			
	Turkey			Switzerland
	Ukraine			UK
Asia	China	Philippines	Hong Kong	Japan
	India	Taiwan	South Korea	Singapore
	Indonesia		Thailand	
	Malaysia			
	Pakistan			
Latin America	Argentina			
	Brazil			
	Central America			
	Chile			
	Colombia			
	Ecuador			

(continued on next page)

Domestic Music Piracy Levels in 2004   *(continued)*

Country	Over 50%	25-50%	10-24%	Less than 10%
	Mexico			
	Paraguay			
	Peru			
	Uruguay			
	Venezuela			
Middle East	Egypt	Israel	Bahrain	
	Kuwait	Oman	Qatar	
	Lebanon	Saudi Arabia	UAE	
Australasia			Australia	
			New Zealand	
Africa	Morocco		Nigeria	
			South Africa	
			Zimbabwe	

Domestic Music piracy levels are calculated as pirate units divided by total expected sales (legal units plus private units.)
Source: IFPI, National Groups

Appendix A.2

Software Industry Piracy Statistics

(from: Second Annual BSA and IDC Global Software Piracy Report, May 2005)

Software Piracy Rankings

20 Countries with the Highest Piracy Rates			20 Countries with the Lowest Piracy Rates		
	2004	2003		2004	2003
Vietnam	92%	92%	United States	21%	22%
Ukraine	91%	91%	New Zealand	23%	23%
China	90%	92%	Austria	25%	27%
Zimbabwe	90%	87%	Sweden	26%	27%
Indonesia	87%	88%	United Kingdom	27%	29%
Russia	87%	87%	Denmark	27%	26%
Nigeria	84%	84%	Switzerland	28%	31%
Tunisia	84%	82%	Japan	28%	29%
Algeria	83%	84%	Finland	29%	31%
Kenya	83%	80%	Germany	29%	30%
Paraguay	83%	83%	Belgium	29%	29%

(continued on next page)

Software Piracy Rankings   *(continued)*

20 Countries with the Highest Piracy Rates			*20 Countries with the Lowest Piracy Rates*		
	2004	*2003*		*2004*	*2003*
Pakistan	82%	83%	Netherlands	30%	33%
Bolivia	80%	78%	Norway	31%	32%
El Salvador	80%	79%	Australia	32%	31%
Nicaragua	80%	79%	Israel	33%	35%
Thailand	70%	80%	UAE	34%	34%
Venezuela	79%	72%	Canada	36%	35%
Guatemala	78%	77%	South Africa	37%	36%
Dominican Republic	77%	76%	Ireland	38%	41%
Lebanon	75%	74%	Portugal	40%	41%

Ranking by 2004 Software Piracy Losses

Piracy of $100 Million or More

	$M		$M
United States	6,645	Sweden	304
China	3,565	Denmark	226
France	2,928	South Africa	196
Germany	2,286	Norway	184
United Kingdom	1,963	Indonesia	183
Japan	1,787	Thailand	183
Italy	1,500	Turkey	182
Russia	1,362	Finland	177
Canada	889	Taiwan	161
Brazil	659	Malaysia	134
Spain	634	Czech Republic	132
Netherlands	628	Austria	128
India	519	Hungary	126
Korea	506	Saudi Arabia	125
Australia	409	Hong Kong	116
Mexico	407	Argentina	108
Poland	379	Ukraine	107
Belgium	309	Greece	106
Switzerland	309		

Appendix B

Organizations Accorded Observer Status at the WIPO (2005)
(adapted from WIPO BIG/158/17 – Annex II)

Inter-governmental organizations – UN system

1 United Nations (UN)
2 International Labour Organization (ILO)
3 Food and Agriculture Organization of the United Nations (FAO)
4 United Nations Educational, Scientific and Cultural Organization (UNESCO)
5 World Health Organization (WHO)
6 International Bank for Reconstruction and Development (IBRD)
7 International Finance Corporation (IFC)
8 International Development Association (IDA)
9 International Monetary Fund (IMF)
10 International Civil Aviation Organization (ICAO)
11 Universal Postal Union (UPU)
12 International Telecommunication Union (ITU)
13 World Meteorological Organization (WMO)
14 International Maritime Organization (IMO)
15 International Fund for Agricultural Development (IFAD)
16 United Nations Industrial Development Organization (UNIDO)
17 International Atomic Energy Agency (IAEA)

Inter-governmental organizations – industrial property

1 African Intellectual Property Organization (OAPI)
2 African Regional Intellectual Property Organization (ARIPO)
3 Arab States Broadcasting Union (ASBU)
4 Benelux Designs Office (BBDM)
5 Benelux Trademark Office (BBM)
6 European Patent Organization (EPO)
7 Eurasian Patent Organization (EAPO)
8 International Union for the Protection of New Varieties of Plants (UPOV)
9 Interstate Council on the Protection of Industrial Property (ICPIP)
10 Patent Office of the Cooperation Council for the Arab States of the Gulf (GCC Patent Office)

Inter-governmental organizations – worldwide

1   Commonwealth of Learning (COL)
2   Commonwealth Secretariat
3   Community of Portuguese-speaking Countries (CPLP)
4   International Criminal Police Organization (INTERPOL)
5   International Institute for the Unification of Private Law
    (UNIDROIT)
6   International Olive Oil Council (IOOC)
7   International Vine and Wine Office (IWO)
8   *Organisation internationale de la Francophonie* (OIF)
9   South Centre
10 World Trade Organization (WTO)

Inter-governmental organizations – regional

1   African, Caribbean and Pacific Group of States (ACP Group)
2   African Regional Centre for Technology (ARCT)
3   African Union (AU)
4   Arab League Educational, Cultural and Scientific Organization
    (ALECSO)
5   Arab Industrial Development and Mining Organization (AIDMO)
6   Asian-African Legal Consultative Committee (AALCC)
7   Association of South East Asian Nations (ASEAN)
8   Caribbean Community (CARICOM)
9   Commission of the European Communities (CEC)
10 Commonwealth Fund for Technical Cooperation (CFTC)
11 Commonwealth of Independent States (CIS)
12 *Communauté économique et monétaire en Afrique centrale* (CEMAC)
13 Conference of Latin American Authorities on Informatics (CALAI)
14 Council of Europe (CE)
15 Economic Community of the Great Lakes Countries (CEPGL)
16 European Free Trade Association (EFTA)
17 European Audiovisual Observatory
18 Federation of Arab Scientific Research Councils (FASRC)
19 General Secretariat of the Andean Community
20 Islamic Educational, Scientific and Cultural Organization
    (ISESCO)
21 Latin American Economic System (SELA)
22 Latin American Integration Association (LAIA)
23 League of Arab States (LAS)
24 Organization of American States (OAS)

25 Organization of the Islamic Conference (OIC)
26 Central American Economic Integration Secretariat
27 *Red de Información Tecnológica Latinoamericana* (RITLA)
28 *Secretaría de Cooperación Iberoamericana* (SECIB)
29 Southern African Development Community

Non-governmental organizations

1 ActionAid
2 Actors, Interpreting Artists Committee (CSAI)
3 Afro-Asian Book Council (AABC)
4 AmSong
5 Arab Society for Intellectual Property (ASIP)
6 ASEAN Intellectual Property Association (ASEAN IPA)
7 Asia & Pacific Internet Association (APIA)
8 Asian Patent Attorneys Association
9 Asia-Pacific Broadcasting Union (ABU)
10 *Association européenne des éditeurs de journaux* (ENPA)
11 *Association européenne pour la protection des œuvres et services cryptés* (AEPOC)
12 Association for the International Collective Management of Audiovisual Works (AGICOA)
13 Association for the Protection of Industrial Property in the Arab World (APPIMAF)
14 Association of Commercial Television in Europe (ACT)
15 Association of European Performers' Organizations (AEPO-ARTIS)
16 Association of European Radios (AER)
17 Association of European Trademark Owners (MARQUES)
18 *Association pour la promotion de la propriété intellectuelle en Afrique* (APPIA)
19 Benelux Association of Trademark and Design Agents (BMM)
20 Biotechnology Industry Organization (BIO)
21 Caribbean Broadcasting Union (CBU)
22 Center for International Environmental Law (CIEL)
23 Central and Eastern European Copyright Alliance (CEECA)
24 Centre for Innovation Law and Policy (the Centre)
25 Centre for International Industrial Property Studies (CEIPI)
26 Civil Society Coalition (CSC)
27 Coalition for Intellectual Property Rights (CIPR)
28 Committee of National Institutes of Intellectual Property Attorneys (CNIPA)
29 Committee of Nordic Industrial Property Agents (CONOPA)

30   Computer Law Association (CLA)
31   *Confédération européenne des producteurs de spiriteux* (CEPS)
32   *Conseil francophone de la chanson* (CFC)
33   Co-ordinating Council of Audiovisual Archives Associations (CCAAA)
34   Coordination of European Independent Producers (CEPI)
35   Coordination of European Picture Agencies-News and Stock (CEPIC)
36   CropLife International
37   Council of European Industrial Federations (CEIF)
38   Digital Media Association (DiMA)
39   Digital Video Broadcasting (DVB)
40   *Entidad de Gestión de Derechos de los Productores Audiovisuales* (EGEDA)
41   European Alliance of Press Agencies (EAPA)
42   European Association of Communications Agencies (EACA)
43   European Brands Association (AIM)
44   European Broadcasting Union (EBU)
45   European Bureau of Library, Information and Documentation Associations (EBLIDA)
46   European Cable Communications Association (ECCA)
47   European Chemical Industry Council (CEFIC)
48   European Committee for Interoperable Systems (ECIS)
49   European Communities Trade Mark Association (ECTA)
50   European Computer Manufacturers Association (ECMA)
51   European Council of American Chambers of Commerce (ECACC)
52   European Crop Protection Association (ECPA)
53   European Federation of Agents of Industry in Industrial Property (FEMIPI)
54   European Federation of Pharmaceutical Industries' Associations (EFPIA)
55   European Film Companies Alliance (EFCA)
56   European Generic Medicines Association (EGA)
57   European Industrial Research Management Association (EIRMA)
58   European Information and Communications Technology Industry Association (EICTA)
59   European Publishers Council (EPC)
60   European Sound Directors Association (ESDA)
61   European Tape Industry Council (ETIC)
62   European Visual Artists (EVA)
63   European Writers' Congress (EWC)
64   Exchange and Cooperation Centre for Latin America (ECCLA)

65   Federation of European Audiovisual Directors (FERA)
66   Federation of Scriptwriters in Europe (FSE)
67   Foundation for a Free Information Infrastructure (FFII.e.V.)
68   Free Software Foundation Europe (FSF Europe)
69   Friends World Committee for Consultation (FWCC)
70   Global Anti-Counterfeiting Group (GACG)
71   Ibero-American Television Organization (OTI)
72   Ibero-Latin-American Federation of Performers (FILAIE)
73   Independent Film and Television Alliance (I.F.T.A)
74   Independent Film Producers International Association (IFPIA)
75   Independent Music Companies Association (IMPALA)
76   *Ingénieurs du Monde* (IdM)
77   Institute for African Development (INADEV)
78   Institute of Professional Representatives Before the European
     Patent Office (EPI)
79   Interactive Software Federation of Europe (ISFE)
80   Inter-American Association of Industrial Property (ASIPI)
81   Inter-American Copyright Institute (IIDA)
82   International Advertising Association (IAA)
83   International Affiliation of Writers' Guilds (IAWG)
84   International Air Transport Association (IATA)
85   International Alliance of Orchestra Associations (IAOA)
86   International Anticounterfeiting Coalition, Inc. (IACC)
87   International Association for Mass Communication Research
     (IAMCR)
88   International Association for the Advancement of Teaching and
     Research in Intellectual Property (ATRIP)
89   International Association for the Protection of Industrial Property
     (AIPPI)
90   International Association of Art (IAA)
91   International Association of Audio-Visual Writers and Directors
     (AIDAA)
92   International Association of Authors of Comics and Cartoons
     (AIAC)
93   International Association of Broadcasting (IAB)
94   International Association of Conference Interpreters (AIIC)
95   International Association of Entertainment Lawyers (IAEL)
96   International Bar Association (IBA)
97   International Bureau of Societies Administering the Rights of
     Mechanical Recording and Reproduction (BIEM)
98   International Chamber of Commerce (ICC)
99   International Commission of Jurists (ICJ)

100   International Communications Round Table (ICRT)
101   International Confederation of Free Trade Unions (ICFTU)
102   International Confederation of Music Publishers (ICMP)
103   International Confederation of Professional and Intellectual Workers (CITI)
104   International Confederation of Societies of Authors and Composers (CISAC)
105   International Cooperation for Development and Solidarity (CIDSE)
106   International Copyright Society (INTERGU)
107   International Council of Graphic Design Associations (ICOGRADA)
108   International Council for Science (ICSU)
109   International Council of Societies of Industrial Design (ICSID)
110   International Council on Archives (ICA)
111   International Dance Council (IDC)
112   International DOI Foundation (IDF)
113   International Federation of Actors (FIA)
114   International Federation of Associations of Film Distributors (FIAD)
115   International Federation of Commercial Arbitration Institutions (IFCAI)
116   International Federation of Computer Law Associations (IFCLA)
117   International Federation of Film Producers Associations (FIAPF)
118   International Federation of Industrial Property Attorneys (FICPI)
119   International Federation of Interior Architects/Interior Designers (IFI)
120   International Federation of Inventors' Associations (IFIA)
121   International Federation of Journalists (IFJ)
122   International Federation of Library Associations and Institutions (IFLA)
123   International Federation of Musicians (FIM)
124   International Federation of Pharmaceutical Manufacturers Associations (IFPMA)
125   International Federation of Press Clipping and Media Monitor Bureaus (FIBEP)
126   International Federation of Reproduction Rights Organizations (IFRRO)
127   International Federation of the Periodical Press (FIPP)
128   International Federation of the Phonographic Industry (IFPI)
129   International Federation of Translators (FIT)
130   International Federation of Wines and Spirits (FIVS)

131 International Franchise Association (IFA)
132 International Group of Scientific, Technical and Medical
     Publishers (STM)
133 International Hotel and Restaurant Association (IHRA)
134 International Institute of Communications (IIC)
135 International Law Association (ILA)
136 International League of Competition Law (LIDC)
137 International Literary and Artistic Association (ALAI)
138 International Music Managers Forum (IMMF)
139 International Organization for Standardization (ISO)
140 International Organization of Hotel and Restaurant Associations
     (HoReCa)
141 International Organization of Journalists (IOJ)
142 International Poetry for Peace Association (IPPA)
143 International Publishers Association (IPA)
144 International Trademark Association (INTA)
145 International Union of Architects (UIA)
146 International Union of Cinemas (UNIC)
147 International Video Federation (IVF)
148 International Wine Law Association (AIDV)
149 International Writers Guild (IWG)
150 Latin American Association of Pharmaceutical Industries
     (ALIFAR)
151 Latin American Federation of Music Publishers (FLADEM)
152 Latin American Institute for Advanced Technology, Computer
     Science and Law (ILATID)
153 Law Association for Asia and the Pacific (LAWASIA)
154 Licensing Executives Society (International) (LES)
155 Max-Planck Institute for Intellectual Property, Competition and
     Tax Law
156 *Médecins Sans Frontières* (MSF)
157 North American Broadcasters Association (NABA)
158 *Organisation ibéro-américaine des droits d'auteur-Latinautor Inc.*
159 Organization for an International Geographical Indications
     Network (ORIGIN)
160 Pacific Industrial Property Association (PIPA)
161 Patent Documentation Group (PDG)
162 Pearle Performing Arts Employers Associations League Europe
163 Rights & Democracy
164 Scandinavian Patent Attorney Society (PS)
165 Software & Information Industry Association (SIIA)
166 The Chartered Institute of Arbitrators (CIArb)

167   The World Conservation Union (IUCN)
168   Union Network International – Media and Entertainment (UNI-MEI)
169   Union of African Journalists (UAJ)
170   Union of European Practitioners in Industrial Property (UNION)
171   Union of Industrial and Employers' Confederations of Europe (UNICE)
172   Union of National Radio and Television Organizations of Africa (URTNA)
173   World Association for Small & Medium Enterprises (WASME)
174   World Association of Newspapers (WAN)
175   World Blind Union (WBU)
176   World Federation for Culture Collections (WFCC)
177   World Federation of Advertisers (WFA)
178   World Federation of Engineering Organizations (WFEO)
179   World Self Medication Industry (WSMI)
180   World Union of Professions (WUP)

National non-governmental organizations

1   American Association for the Advancement of Science (AAAS)
2   American Intellectual Property Law Association (AIPLA)
3   *Association nationale des artistes interprètes* (ANDI)
4   *Association brésilienne des émetteurs de radio et de télévision* (ABERT)
5   *Association Bouregreg* (BOUREGREG)
6   British Copyright Council (BCC)
7   Copyright Research and Information Center (CRIC)
8   Creators' Rights Alliance (CRA)
9   Electronic Frontier Foundation (EFF)
10   Japan Institute of Invention and Innovation (JIII)
11   Picture Archive Council of America (PACA)
12   *Sociedade Portuguesa de Autores* (SPA)
13   South African Institute of Intellectual Property Law (SAIIPL)

Appendix C

WIPO Statistics; Filing of PCT International Applications

PCT Filing – Percentage by Origin, as at April 2005
(adapted from WIPO Statistics: PCT Statistical Indicators Report;
Annual Statistics 1978–2004, as at April 2005)

Explanations and definitions:

- The table shows the percentage of all PCT applications filed by the top countries or regions of origin.
- EPC member states are the 30 member states of the European Patent Convention. They are reported individually and as a group.
- All origins with more than 1,000 applications in 2004 are shown.

	1990	*1995*	*2000*	*2004*
EPC States	43.5%	42.1%	38.5%	35.9%
USA	39.0%	42.8%	40.8%	35.3%
Japan	8.8%	6.9%	10.3%	16.6%
Germany	13.9%	12.8%	13.5%	12.5%
France	5.1%	4.7%	4.4%	4.3%
GB	9.9%	7.5%	5.1%	4.1%
Netherlands	1.4%	3.5%	3.1%	3.4%
Rep. of Korea	0.1%	0.5%	1.7%	2.9%
Switzerland	2.0%	2.2%	2.1%	2.3%
Sweden	4.4%	3.9%	3.3%	2.3%
Italy	1.2%	1.4%	1.5%	1.8%
Canada	2.5%	2.1%	1.9%	1.7%
Australia	3.1%	2.2%	1.7%	1.5%
China	0.0%	0.3%	0.8%	1.4%
Finland	1.6%	1.8%	1.7%	1.4%
Israel	0.0%	0.5%	1.0%	1.0%
Denmark	1.7%	1.4%	0.9%	0.9%
All Others	3.0%	2.6%	3.3%	3.6%

WIPO Statistics; Filing of PCT International Applications

PCT – Developing Countries by quantity of filings, as at April 2005
(adapted from WIPO Statistics: PCT Statistical Indicators Report;
Annual Statistics 1978–2004, as at April 2005)

Explanation and definition:

• The table shows the number of applications filed by applicants
  from the top 10 developing countries.

	1990	1995	2000	2004
Rep. of Korea	24	196	1,580	3,554
China	0	103	784	1,705
South Africa	1	42	387	404
India	0	0	190	689
Singapore	0	26	222	423
Brazil	22	67	178	278
Mexico	0	11	73	118
Cyprus	2	3	19	39
Malaysia	0	2	5	45
Colombia	0	2	4	22

Notes

Foreword

1   Christopher May, *A Global Political Economy of Intellectual Property Rights: The New Enclosures?* (London: Routledge, 2000).

2   As Steve Hughes demonstrates in his forthcoming book in the series, the International Labor Organization (ILO) – a body that also traces its antecedents to the emergence of transnational regulation in the nineteenth century – is one of the few other organizations to exude these qualities. See also Steve Hughes, "Coming in from the Cold: Labour, the ILO and the International Labour Standards Regime," in Rorden Wilkinson and Steve Hughes, eds., *Global Governance: Critical Perspectives* (London: Routledge, 2002); and Rorden Wilkinson, "Peripheralising Labour: The ILO, WTO and the Completion of the Bretton Woods Project," in Jeffery Harrod and Robert O'Brien (eds.), *Globalized Unions? Theory and Strategies of Organized Labour in the Global Political Economy* (London: Routledge, 2002).

3   See Craig N. Murphy, *International Organisation and Industrial Change: Global Governance since 1850* (Cambridge: Polity Press, 1994).

1   Intellectual Property

1   See for instance: Alice D. Ba and Matthew J. Hoffmann, *Contending Perspectives on Global Governance: Coherence, Contestation and World Order* (London: Routledge, 2005); Michael Barnett and Raymond Duvall, eds., *Power in Global Governance* (Cambridge: Cambridge University Press, 2005); Robert O'Brien, Anne Marie Goetz, Jan Aart Scholte and Marc Williams, *Contesting Global Governance: Multilateral Economic Institutions and Global Social Movements* (Cambridge: Cambridge University Press, 2000); and Rorden Wilkinson and Steve Hughes, eds., *Global Governance: Critical Perspectives* (London: Routledge, 2002), to mention merely four recent treatments, that have little if anything to say about the WIPO. While the organization is mentioned a number of times in Kees van der Pijl, Libby Assassi and Duncan Wigan, eds.., *Global Regulation: Managing Crises After the Imperial Turn* (Basingstoke, England: Palgrave Macmillan, 2004) all but one of these references appear in my own chapter.

2   Anne-Marie Slaughter, *A New World Order* (Princeton: Princeton University Press, 2004). Likewise, Abram Chayes and Antonia Handler Chayes, *The New Sovereignty: Compliance with International Regulatory Agreements* (Cambridge, Mass.: Harvard University Press, 1995), a widely cited and highly regarded study of major shifts

in global governance, only mentions the WIPO in a table of UN specialized agencies in an appendix after the main text.

3 See for instance: Peter Dicken, *Global Shift: Reshaping the Global Economic Map in the Twentieth Century*, fourth edition (London: Sage Publications, 2003); Robert Gilpin, *Global Political Economy: Understanding International Economic Order* (Princeton: Princeton University Press, 2001); Jonathan Michie, ed., *The Handbook of Globalization* (Cheltenham, England: Edward Elgar, 2001); Nicola Phillips, ed., *Globalizing International Political Economy* (Basingstoke, England: Palgrave Macmillan, 2005); John Ravenhill, ed., *Global Political Economy* (Oxford: Oxford University Press, 2005), all of which while excellent works in their own right, have only passing mentions of the WIPO, if the organization is mentioned at all.

4 Christopher May, *The Information Society: A Sceptical View* (Cambridge: Polity Press, 2002).

5 The (highly contested) figures on the extent and geographical spread of piracy in the music and software industries are included in appendix A.

6 John Braithwaite and Peter Drahos, *Global Business Regulation* (Cambridge: Cambridge University Press, 2000), 61–64.

7 Arnold Plant, "The Economic Theory Concerning Patents for Inventions," *Economica* 1 (February 1934): 30–51, at 31.

8 Christopher May, *A Global Political Economy of Intellectual Property Rights: The New Enclosures?* (London: Routledge, 2000), chapter one.

9 John Locke, *Two Treatises on Government* (Cambridge: Cambridge University Press, 1690 [reprinted 1988]).

10 Georg Hegel, *Philosophy of Right* (Oxford: Oxford University Press, 1821, reprinted 1967).

11 May, *A Global Political Economy of Intellectual Property Rights*, 18–21.

12 Douglass C. North, *Institutions, Institutional Change and Economic Performance* (Cambridge: Cambridge University Press, 1990), 34–35.

2   The WIPO's Antecedents and History

1 The term "intellectual property" as a collective noun also emerged around this time, having no currency in the previous four hundred years of the history of the laws of patent and copyright.

2 Elements of this chapter are drawn from Christopher May and Susan Sell, *Intellectual Property Rights: A Critical History* (Boulder, Colo.: Lynne Rienner Publishers, 2005), chapters five and six.

3 Fritz Malchup and Edith Penrose, "The Patent Controversy in the Nineteenth Century," *The Journal of Economic History* 10, no. 1 (May 1950): 1–29, at 4–6.

4 Moureen Coulter, *Property in Ideas: The Patent Question in Mid-Victorian Britain* (Kirksville, Miss.: Thomas Jefferson University Press, 1991), 176.

5 Graham Dutfield, *Intellectual Property and the Life Sciences Industries: A Twentieth Century History* (Aldershot, England: Dartmouth Publishing Co., 2003), 55.

6 Ruth Gana, "Has Creativity Died in the Third World? Some Implications of the Internationalization of Intellectual Property," *Denver Journal of International Law & Policy* 24, no. 1 (1995): 109–44, at 137.

7 Aubert Clark, *The Movement for International Copyright in Nineteenth Century America* (Westport, Conn.: Greenwood Press, 1960), 134; Paul Goldstein, *Copyright's Highway: From Gutenberg to the Celestial Jukebox* (New York: Hill and Wang, 1994), 181–82.

8 Sam Ricketson, *The Berne Convention for the Protection of Literary and Artistic Works: 1886–1986* (London: Kluwer/Centre for Commercial Law Studies, 1987), 49ff.

9 Gana, "Has Creativity Died in the Third World?", 137.

10 John Feather, *Publishing, Piracy and Politics: An Historical Study of Copyright in Britain* (London: Mansell Publishing Limited, 1994), 168.

11 Carla Hesse, "The Rise of Intellectual Property, 700 B.C. – A.D. 2000: An Idea in the Balance," *Daedalus* 131, no. 2 (Spring 2002): 26–45, at 42.

12 World Intellectual Property Organization, *Introduction to Intellectual Property Theory and Practice* (London: Kluwer Law International 1997), 4.

13 Peter Drahos, "States and Intellectual Property: The Past, the Present and the Future" in: David Saunders and Brad Sherman, eds., *From Berne to Geneva: Recent Developments in International Copyright and Neighboring Rights* (Nathan, Queensland: Australian Key Centre for Culture and Media Policy, 1997), 47–70.

14 Craig N. Murphy, *International Organization and Industrial Change: Global Governance Since 1850* (Cambridge: Polity Press, 1994), chapter two and *passim*.

15 Vincent Porter, *Beyond the Berne Convention: Copyright, Broadcasting and the Single European Market* (London: John Libbey, 1991), 4.

16 Porter, *Beyond the Berne Convention*, 7.

17 Porter, *Beyond the Berne Convention,* 22.

18 Andréa Koury Menescal, "Changing WIPO's Ways? The 2004 Development Agenda in Historical Perspective," *Journal of World Intellectual Property* 8, part 6 (2005): 761–96.

19 Sisule F. Musungu and Graham Dutfield, *Multilateral Agreements and a TRIPs-Plus World: The World Intellectual Property Organization* (TRIPs Issue Papers: 3) (Geneva, Switzerland: Quaker United Nations Office, 2003), 4.

20 Arpad Bogsch, *The First Twenty-Five Years of the World Intellectual Property Organization from 1967 to 1992* (WIPO Publication No. 881 [E]) (Geneva, Switzerland: International Bureau of Intellectual Property, 1992), 22.

21 Musungu and Dutfield, *Multilateral Agreements and a TRIPs-Plus World*, 4.

22 Bogsch, *The First Twenty-Five Years of the World Intellectual Property Organization*, 28.

23 Michael P. Ryan, *Knowledge Diplomacy: Global Competition and the Politics of Intellectual Property* (Washington DC: Brookings Institution Press, 1998), 127.

24 Susan K. Sell, *Power and Ideas: North-South Politics of Intellectual Property and Antitrust* (Albany: State University of New York Press, 1998), 116.

25 Bogsch, *The First Twenty-Five Years of the World Intellectual Property Organization*, 28.

26 World Intellectual Property Organization, *Records of the Intellectual Property Conference of Stockholm, June 11 to July 14, 1967* (minutes for the meeting to create WIPO) (Geneva, Switzerland: WIPO, 1967), 830.

27 The Convention is available on the Union of International Associations website; http://www.uia.org/legal/app51.php (15 June 2005).

28 Peter Drahos and John Braithwaite, *Information Feudalism: Who Owns the Knowledge Economy?* (London: Earthscan Publications, 2002), 113.

29 Agreement between the United Nations and the World Intellectual Property Organization, available at http://www.wipo.int/treaties/en/agreement (19 December 2005).

30 World Intellectual Property Organization, *Report of the World Intellectual Property Organization to the Economic and Social Council of the United Nations at its Fifty-Ninth*

Session (Analytical Summary for the year 1974) (Geneva, Switzerland: WIPO, 1975), 13.

31 WIPO, *Report of the World Intellectual Property Organization to the Economic and Social Council of the United Nations*, 15.

32 Susan K. Sell, *Private Power, Public Law. The Globalization of Intellectual Property Rights* (Cambridge: Cambridge University Press, 2003), chapter five.

33 Christopher May, *The Information Society: A Sceptical View* (Cambridge: Polity Press, 2002).

34 The report is discussed in Peter Drahos, "Developing Countries and Intellectual Property Standard-Setting," *Journal of World Intellectual Property* 5, no. 5 (2002): 765–89, at 768.

35 Drahos, "Developing Countries and Intellectual Property Standard-Setting", 774–75; Duncan Matthews, *Globalizing Intellectual Property Rights: The TRIPs Agreement* (London: Routledge, 2002), 31–33.

36 Christopher May, *A Global Political Economy of Intellectual Property Rights: The New Enclosures?* (London: Routledge, 2000), 88.

37 Drahos and Braithwaite, *Information Feudalism*, 134.

38 Matthews, *Globalizing Intellectual Property Rights*, 33.

39 Extended discussions of the negotiations that led to TRIPs can be found in Matthews, *Globalizing Intellectual Property Rights*, chapter two; and Terence P. Stewart, *The GATT Uruguay Round: A Negotiating History (1986–1992)* (Deventer, Boston: Kluwer Law and Taxation Publishers 1993), 2245–2333.

40 Sell, *Power and Ideas*, chapter four.

41 Sell, *Power and Ideas*, 116.

42 Adronico Oduogo Adede, "Origins and History of the TRIPs Negotiations," in: Christophe Bellmann, Graham Dutfield and Ricardo Meléndez-Ortiz, eds., *Trading in Knowledge: Development Perspectives on TRIPs, Trade and Sustainability* (London: Earthscan, 2003), 23–35, at 32–34.

43 Stewart, *The GATT Uruguay Round: A Negotiating History*, 2287; 2313.

44 Laurence R. Hefler, "Regime Shifting: The TRIPs Agreement and New Dynamics of International Intellectual Property Lawmaking," *Yale Journal of International Law* 29, no. 1 (2004): 1–83, at 18, footnote 70.

45 Hefler, "Regime Shifting," 21–22.

46 G. Bruce Doern, *Global Change and Intellectual Property Agencies: An Institutional Perspective* (London: Pinter Publishers, 1999), chapter eight.

47 Available at http://www.wipo.int/treaties/en/agreement/trtdocs_wo030.html (19 December 2005).

48 Graham Dutfield, *Intellectual Property, Biogenetic Resources and Traditional Knowledge* (London: Earthscan, 2004), 133.

3 How the WIPO Works

1 World Intellectual Property Organization, *Introduction to Intellectual Property Theory and Practice* (London: Kluwer Law International 1997), 30.

2 WIPO, *Introduction to Intellectual Property Theory and Practice*, 42.

3 A full list of all 259 observers can be found in appendix B.

4 WIPO, *Introduction to Intellectual Property Theory and Practice*, 29.

5 Michael P. Ryan, *Knowledge Diplomacy: Global Competition and the Politics of Intellectual Property* (Washington DC: Brookings Institution Press, 1998), 128.

6 Keith E. Maskus, *Intellectual Property Rights in the Global Economy* (Washington DC: Institute for International Economics, 2000), 67–68.

7 World Intellectual Property Organization, *The International Patent System in 2004: Yearly Review of the PCT* (Geneva: WIPO, 2004), 3.

8 WIPO, *The International Patent System in 2004*, 6.

9 Tables of current and historic levels of patent applications through the PCT can be found in appendix C.

10 World Intellectual Property Organization, *Annual Report* (Geneva, Switzerland: WIPO, 2003), 13.

11 WIPO, *Annual Report* 2003, 15.

12 G. Bruce Doern, *Global Change and Intellectual Property Agencies: An Institutional Perspective* (London: Pinter Publishers, 1999), 44.

13 WIPO, *Introduction to Intellectual Property Theory and Practice*, 32–3.

14 World Intellectual Property Organization, "Assistance in the Field of Intellectual Property Legislation," available at http://www.wipo.int/cfdiplaw/en/assistance_ip. htm (12 September 2002, but now not available in this form) (emphasis added).

15 WIPO, "Assistance in the Field of Intellectual Property Legislation"; at the time of writing more recent detailed figures were unavailable.

16 WIPO, *Annual Report* 2003, 5.

17 WIPO, *Annual Report* 2003, 5–7.

18 Christopher May and Susan Sell, *Intellectual Property Rights: A Critical History* (Boulder, Colo.: Lynne Rienner Publishers, 2005).

19 Richard H. Steinberg, "In the Shadow of Law or Power? Consensus-Based Bargaining in the GATT/WTO," *International Organization* 56, no. 2 (Spring 2002): 339–74.

20 Kurt Burch, *"Property" and the Making of the International System* (Boulder, Colo.: Lynne Rienner, 1998), 215.

21 A. Samuel Oddi, "TRIPS – Natural Rights and a 'Polite Form of Economic Imperialism'," *Vanderbilt Journal of Transnational Law* 29 (1996): 415–70, at 440.

22 Deborah J. Halbert, *Intellectual Property in the Information Age: The Politics of Expanding Ownership Rights* (Westport, Conn.: Quorum Books, 1999), 85–94.

23 Howard C. Anawalt, "International Intellectual Property, Progress and the Rule of Law," *Santa Clara Computer and High Technology Law Journal* 19, no. 2 (2003): 383–405, at 401.

24 Space precludes a detailed account of TRIPs' numerous sections; Maskus, *Intellectual Property Rights in the Global Economy*, chapter two, offers a good concise summary of the agreement, as does Duncan Matthews, *Globalizing Intellectual Property Rights: The TRIPs Agreement* (London: Routledge, 2002), chapter three, but also see the treatment in May and Sell, *Intellectual Property Rights*, chapter seven.

25 Frederick M. Abbott, "Distributed Governance at the WTO-WIPO: An Evolving Model for Open-Architecture Integrated Governance," *Journal of International Economic Law* 3, no. 1 (March 2000): 63–82, at 69.

26 Laurence R. Hefler, "Regime Shifting: The TRIPs Agreement and New Dynamics of International Intellectual Property Lawmaking," *Yale Journal of International Law* 29, no. 1 (2004): 1–83, at 26 (references removed).

27 Graham Dutfield, *Intellectual Property, Biogenetic Resources and Traditional Knowledge* (London: Earthscan, 2004); Hefler, "Regime Shifting", 26–52.

4   Global Governance and Intellectual Property

1 Craig N. Murphy, *International Organization and Industrial Change: Global Governance Since 1850* (Cambridge: Polity Press, 1994).

2 Space precludes a full discussion of the political economy of ICANN, however the account in Milton L. Mueller, *Ruling the Root: Internet Governance and the Taming of Cyberspace* (Cambridge, Mass.: MIT Press, 2002), chapters 8–10, is clear and well informed.

3 Frederick M. Abbott, "Distributed Governance at the WTO-WIPO: An Evolving Model for Open-Architecture Integrated Governance," *Journal of International Economic Law* 3, no. 1 (March 2000): 63–82.

4 Edward Kwakwa, "Some Comments on Rulemaking at the World Intellectual Property Organization," *Duke Journal of Comparative and International Law* 12, no. 1 (2001): 179–96, at 191–92.

5 Robert Shaw, "Internet Domain Names: Whose Domain is This?" in: Brian Kahin and James H. Keller, eds., *Coordinating the Internet* (Cambridge, Mass.: MIT Press, 1997), 107–34, at 107.

6 Shaw, "Internet Domain Names," 110.

7 Carl Oppedahl, "Trademark Disputes in the Assignment of Domain Names" in: Brian Kahin and James H. Keller, eds., *Coordinating the Internet* (Cambridge, Mass.: MIT Press, 1997), 154–86, at 160.

8 Shaw, "Internet Domain Names," 113.

9 The early history of trademark-related domain name disputes is discussed in Oppedahl, "Trademark Disputes in the Assignment of Domain Names," while discussion of a number of specific early disputes can be found in Gayle Weiswasser, "Domain Names, the Internet and Trademarks: Infringement in Cyberspace," *Santa Clara Computer and High Technology Law Journal* 13 (1997): 137–80.

10 Leslie A. Pal and Tatyana Teplova, "Domain Names: Global Governance of the Internet" in: E. Lynn Oliver and Larry Sanders, eds., *E-Government Reconsidered: Renewal of Governance for the Knowledge Age* (Regina: Canadian Plains Research Center/University of Regina, 2004), 43–58, at 47.

11 William A. Foster, "Registering the Domain Name System: An Exercise in Global Decision Making" in: Brian Kahin and James H. Keller, eds., *Coordinating the Internet* (Cambridge, Mass.: MIT Press, 1997), 194–207.

12 Charlotte Waelde, "Trade Marks and Domain Names: There's a Lot in a Name" in: Lillian Edwards and Charlotte Waelde, eds., *Law and the Internet: A Framework for Electronic Commerce* (Second Edition) (Oxford: Hart Publishing, 2000), 133–70, at 156–57. The consultation process itself is described at length by Michael Froomkin, "Semi-Private International Rule-making: Lessons Learned from the WIPO Domain Name Process" in: Christopher Marsden, ed., *Regulating the Information Society* (London: Routledge, 2000), 211–32, at 218–30; the author was one of the civil society participants.

13 Graeme B. Dinwoodie, "The Architecture of the International Intellectual Property System," *Chicago-Kent Law Review* 77, no. 3 (2002): 993–1014, at 1001 [fns. del].

14 Mueller, *Ruling the Root*, 191–92.

15 Waelde, "Trade Marks and Domain Names," 160.

16 Pal and Teplova, "Domain Names," 32.

17 Study by Milton Mueller cited in Yee Fen Lim, "Internet Governance, Resolving the Unresolvable: Trademark Law and Internet Domain Names," *International Review of Law, Computers and Technology* 16, no. 2 (2002): 199–209, at 206.

18 Dirk Lehmkuhl, "The Resolution of Domain Name vs. Trademark Conflicts: A Case Study on Regulation beyond the Nation State, and Related Problems," *Zeitschrift für Rechtssoziologie* 23, no. 1 (2002): 61–78, at 71.

19 Peter K. Yu, "Currents and Cross Currents in the International Intellectual Property Regime," *Loyola of Los Angeles Law Review* 38 (2004): 323–443, at 404.

20 Mueller, *Ruling the Root*, 226.

21 World Intellectual Property Organization, *Annual Report* (Geneva, Switzerland: WIPO, 2003), 16.

22 Kwakwa, "Some Comments on Rulemaking at the World Intellectual Property Organization," 192.

23 This section draws on the analysis developed in Christopher May, "Capacity Building and the (Re)production of Intellectual Property Rights," *Third World Quarterly* 25, no. 5 (2004): 821–37.

24 See, for instance, the half paragraph "discussion" in World Intellectual Property Organization, "Establishing IP Institutions in the Least Developed Countries," *WIPO Magazine* (July–April, 2004), 8–11, at 9. Also see the discussion of the WIPO's website and its presentation of various "myths" about the relationship between public health and TRIPs in Sisule F. Musungu and Graham Dutfield, *Multilateral Agreements and a TRIPs-Plus World: The World Intellectual Property Organization* (TRIPs Issue Papers: 3) (Geneva, Switzerland: Quaker United Nations Office, 2003), 23.

25 Musungu and Dutfield, *Multilateral Agreements and a TRIPs-Plus World*, 23.

26 Graeme B. Dinwoodie, "The Integration of International and Domestic Intellectual Property Lawmaking," *Columbia VLA Journal of Law and the Arts*, 23 no. 3–4 (2000): 307–14, at 311–12 (emphasis added).

27 Peter Drahos and John Braithwaite, *Information Feudalism: Who Owns the Knowledge Economy?* (London: Earthscan Publications, 2002), 101.

28 Michael Finger and Peter Schuler, "Implementation of Uruguay Round Commitments: The Development Challenge," paper presented to the WTO/World Bank Conference on Developing Countries in a Millennium Round, Geneva (20–21 September 1999), 20.

29 WIPO, *Annual Report* 2003, 21.

30 Stephen Gill, *Power and Resistance in the New World Order* (Basingstoke, England: Palgrave Macmillan, 2003), 132.

31 Gill, *Power and Resistance in the New World Order*, 196.

32 Gill, *Power and Resistance in the New World Order*, 177.

33 Jörg Reinbothe and Silke von Lewinski, "The WIPO Treaties 1996: Ready to Come into Force," *European Intellectual Property Review* 24, no. 4 (April 2002): 199–208, at 200.

34 Drahos and Braithwaite, *Information Feudalism*, 184; I have discussed the political economy of DRM elsewhere: see Christopher May, "Digital Rights Management and the Breakdown of Social Norms," *First Monday* 8, no. 11 (November 2003), available at: http://firstmonday.org/issues/issues8_11/may/index.html (21 November 2005).

35 Reinbothe and von Lewinski, "The WIPO Treaties 1996," 201.

36 Oliver Morgan, *International Protection of Performers' Rights* (Oxford: Hart Publishing 2002), 197–99; Reinbothe and von Lewinski, "The WIPO Treaties 1996," 201.

37 Reinbothe and von Lewinski, "The WIPO Treaties 1996," 208.

38 World Intellectual Property Organization, *WIPO Patent Agenda: Options for Development of the International Patent System* document A/37/6 [19 August] (Geneva: WIPO, 2002).

39 Musungu and Dutfield, *Multilateral Agreements and a TRIPs-Plus World*, 13.

40 Commission on Intellectual Property Rights, *Integrating Intellectual Property Rights and Development Policy* (London: CIPR/Department for International Development, 2002), 133.

41 Musungu and Dutfield, *Multilateral Agreements and a TRIPs-Plus World*, 12.

42 Carlos M. Correa and Sisule F. Musungu, *The WIPO Patent Agenda: The Risks for Developing Countries* (T.R.A.D.E. working paper no. 12) (Geneva, Switzerland: South Centre, 2002), 6–7.

43 Correa and Musungu, *The WIPO Patent Agenda*, 15–22.

44 Biswajit Dhar and R. V. Anuradha, "Substantive Patent Law Treaty; What It Means for India," *Economic and Political Weekly* (26 March 2005): 1346–54, at 1351.

45 Dhar and Anuradha, "Substantive Patent Law Treaty," 1348.

5   The "Problem" with the WIPO

1 Peter Drahos, "Developing Countries and Intellectual Property Standard-Setting," *Journal of World Intellectual Property* 5, no. 5 (2002): 765–89.

2 Drahos, "Developing Countries and Intellectual Property Standard-Setting", 785.

3 Edward Kwakwa, "Some Comments on Rulemaking at the World Intellectual Property Organization," *Duke Journal of Comparative and International Law* 12, no. 1 (2001): 179–96, at 193.

4 Arpad Bogsch, *The First Twenty-Five Years of the World Intellectual Property Organization from 1967 to 1992* (WIPO Publication No. 881 [E]) (Geneva, Switzerland: International Bureau of Intellectual Property, 1992).

5 World Intellectual Property Organization, "Vision and Strategic Direction of WIPO," *WIPO Magazine* (September 1999): 8–9.

6 Kwakwa, "Some Comments on Rulemaking at the World Intellectual Property Organization," 193.

7 Much of this section draws on the work of Sisule Musungu (South Center) and William New (IP Watch), both of whom have been keen observers of the political debates around the Development Agenda, and therefore in addition to the explicit citations in the text, I am grateful to both for their regular updates on this and related issues.

8 Commission on Intellectual Property Rights, *Integrating Intellectual Property Rights and Development Policy* (London: CIPR/Department for International Development, 2002).

9 Sisule F. Musungu, "The WIPO Assemblies 2004: A Review of the Outcomes," *South Bulletin* 89 (15 October 2004): 1–5.

10 Martin Khor, "Strong Support from Developing Countries for Development Agenda at WIPO Assembly," *Third World Network: Info Service on WTO and Trade Issues* (5 October 2004), available from http://www.twnside.org.sg/title2/twninfo165.htm (21 December 2005); The Geneva Declaration on the Future of WIPO was reproduced in the *South Bulletin* 88 (30 September 2004).

11 The WIPO Development Agenda was reproduced in the *South Bulletin* 88 (30 September 2004) and all quotes are taken from this source.

12 Quoted in: Sisule F. Musungu, "A Review of the Outcomes of WIPO Discussions on the Development Agenda Proposal," *Bridges* 8, 9 (October 2004): 21–22.

13 See the elaboration reproduced in *South Bulletin* 101 (15 April 2005).

14 See the proposal reproduced in *South Bulletin* 101 (15 April 2005).

15 Andréa Koury Menescal "Changing WIPO's Ways? The 2004 Development Agenda in Historical Perspective," *Journal of World Intellectual Property* 8, part 6 (2005): 761–96.

16 Christopher May and Susan Sell, *Intellectual Property Rights: A Critical History* (Boulder, Colo.: Lynne Rienner Publishers, 2005), chapter seven.

17 From paragraph 27 of the revised agenda published in *South Bulletin* 101 (15 April 2005).

18 Anonymous source quoted in William New, "Industry Concerned About Development Agenda at WIPO," *Intellectual Property Watch* (2005), available from http://www.ip-watch.org/weblog/wp-trackback.php/125 (8 November 2005).

19 Space precludes a full discussion of all the various proposals, but an overview can be found in Sisule F. Musungu, *Rethinking Innovation, Development and Intellectual Property in the UN: WIPO and Beyond* (TRIPS Issue Papers: 5) (Geneva, Switzerland: Quaker United Nations Office, 2005), section 3.2.1.

20 This author's personal conversation with F. Scott Kieff (Florence, October 2005); Eric Smith, International Intellectual Property Alliance, quoted in New, "Industry Concerned about Development Agenda at WIPO."

21 Musungu, *Rethinking Innovation, Development and Intellectual Property in the UN*, 8.

22 William New, "Debate Heats Up over WIPO Development Agenda," *Intellectual Property Watch* (2005), available from http://www.ip-watch.org/weblog/wp-trackback.php/39 (1 April 2005).

23 William New, "Reform Debate Trips Up WIPO Development Aid Meeting," *Intellectual Property Watch* (2005), available from http://www.ip-watch.org/weblog/wp-trackback.php/45 (15 April 2005); World Intellectual Property Organization, "Results of the 2005 Assemblies of WIPO member states", *WIPO Magazine* (November–December 2005), 2–5, at 3.

24 Sisule F. Musungu and Graham Dutfield, *Multilateral Agreements and a TRIPs-Plus World: The World Intellectual Property Organization* (TRIPs Issue Papers: 3) (Geneva, Switzerland: Quaker United Nations Office, 2003), 19.

25 William New, "Non-Profits, Industry Offers Views on WIPO Development Agenda," *Intellectual Property Watch* (2005), available from http://www.ip-watch.org/weblog/wp-trackback.php/44 (14 April 2005).

26 Menescal, "Changing WIPO's Ways?".

27 William New, "Europe Calls for Continuation of the WIPO Development Agenda Talks," *Intellectual Property Watch* (2005), available from http://www.ip-watch.org/weblog/wp-trackback.php/82 (27 July 2005).

28 William New, "New Committee for WIPO Development Agenda; Patents Reinvigorated," *Intellectual Property Watch* (2005), available from http://www.ip-watch.org/weblog/wp-trackback.php/97 (4 October 2005).

29 This section reflects the situation at the end of 2005.

30 Musungu and Dutfield, *Multilateral Agreements and a TRIPs-Plus World*, 19.

31 Musungu and Dutfield, *Multilateral Agreements and a TRIPs-Plus World*, 19–20.

32 Musungu, "The WIPO Assemblies 2004."

33 Musungu and Dutfield, *Multilateral Agreements and a TRIPs-Plus World*, 20.

34 May and Sell, *Intellectual Property Rights*.

35 Gillian Davies, *Copyright and the Public Interest* (Second Edition) (London: Sweet and Maxwell, 2003), 359.

36 James Boyle, "A Manifesto on WIPO and the Future of Intellectual Property," *South Bulletin* 88 (30 September 2004): 10–17 at 11.

37 Boyle, "A Manifesto on WIPO and the Future of Intellectual Property," 14.

38 Musungu and Dutfield, *Multilateral Agreements and a TRIPs-Plus World*, 21.

39 See for instance, Nitya Nanda, "WIPO Patent Agenda: As If TRIPs Was Not Enough," *Economic and Political Weekly* 39, no. 39 (25 September 2004): 4310–15.

40 Peter K. Yu, "Currents and Cross Currents in the International Intellectual Property Regime," *Loyola of Los Angeles Law Review* 38 (2004): 323–443, at 385.

41 Robert Hunter Wade, "What Strategies are Viable for Developing Countries Today? The World Trade Organisation and the Shrinking of 'Development Space'," *Review of International Political Economy* 10, no. 4 (November 2003): 621–44, at 624.

42 Drahos, "Developing Countries and Intellectual Property Standard-Setting," 777.

43 Vandana Shiva, *Protect or Plunder? Understanding Intellectual Property Rights* (London: Zed Books 2001), 49–68.

44 Daniel J. Gervais, "The Internationalisation of Intellectual Property: New Challenges from the Very Old and the Very New," *Fordham Intellectual Property Media and Entertainment Journal* 12, no. 4 (2002): 929–90.

45 Peter Drahos and John Braithwaite, *Information Feudalism: Who Owns the Knowledge Economy?* (London: Earthscan Publications, 2002), 75.

46 Joost Pauwelyn, "The Role of Public International Law in the WTO: How Far Can We Go?", *American Journal of International Law* 95, no. 3 (July 2001): 535–78 at 577.

47 Daya Shanker, "Legitimacy and the TRIPs Agreement", *Journal of World Intellectual Property* 6, no. 1 (2003): 155–89.

48 Shanker, "Legitimacy and the TRIPs Agreement," 177.

49 Gautam Sen, "The United States and the GATT/WTO System" in: Rosemary Foot, S. Neil MacFarlane and Michael Mastanduno, eds., *US Hegemony and International Organisations* (Oxford: Oxford University Press, 2003): 115–38 at 128; Shanker, "Legitimacy and the TRIPs Agreement," 186.

6 The WIPO's Rise, Fall and Comeback

1 See Laurence R. Hefler, "Regime Shifting: The TRIPs Agreement and New Dynamics of International Intellectual Property Lawmaking", *Yale Journal of International Law* 29, no. 1 (2004): 1–83, for a well developed iteration of this argument, although his suggestion that it is non-governmental actors that are partly driving this process is far from self-evident and has been subject to some adverse comment in private conversations between myself and other researchers.

2 Peter K. Yu, "Currents and Cross Currents in the International Intellectual Property Regime," *Loyola of Los Angeles Law Review* 38 (2004): 323–443, at 428.

3 Hefler, "Regime Shifting."

4 See list of INGOs accorded observer status in appendix B.

5 Sisule F. Musungu and Graham Dutfield, *Multilateral Agreements and a TRIPs-Plus World: The World Intellectual Property Organization* (TRIPs Issue Papers: 3) (Geneva, Switzerland: Quaker United Nations Office, 2003), 22.

6 See the latest budget figures for the WIPO available at http://www.wipo.int/documents/en/document/govbody/budget/2004_05/pdf/wo_pbc_7_2_part_a.pdf (22 December 2005).

7 Graham Dutfield, *Intellectual Property, Biogenetic Resources and Traditional Knowledge* (London: Earthscan, 2004), part three; Michael Finger and Philip Schuler, eds.,

Poor People's Knowledge: Promoting Intellectual Property in Developing Countries (Washington DC: World Bank, 2004).

8 Christopher May, "The Hypocrisy of Forgetfulness: The Contemporary Significance of Early Innovations in Intellectual Property," *Review of International Political Economy* 14, no. 2 (February 2007) (*forthcoming*).

9 See Finger and Schuler, *Poor People's Knowledge*.

10 Peter M. Gerhart, "Distributive Values and Institutional Design in the Provision of Global Public Goods" in: Keith E. Maskus and Jerome H. Reichman, eds., *International Public Goods and Transfer of Technology under a Globalized Intellectual Property Regime* (Cambridge: Cambridge University Press, 2005) 69–77, at 72.

11 Richard Higgott and Morten Ougaard, "Introduction: Beyond System and Society – Towards a Global Polity" in: Richard Higgot and Morten Ougaard, eds., *Towards a Global Polity* (London: Routledge, 2002), 1–13, at 12.

12 Graeme B. Dinwoodie, "The Architecture of the International Intellectual Property System," *Chicago-Kent Law Review* 77, no. 3 (2002): 993–1014, at 1004.

13 Pamela Samuleson, "Innovation and Competition: Conflicts Over Intellectual Property Rights in New Technologies" in: Vivian Weill and John W. Snapper, eds., *Owning Scientific and Technical Information – Value and Ethical Issues* (New Brunswick, N.J.: Rutgers University Press, 1989), 169–92, at 179 (emphasis added).

Further Reading

Bogsch, Arpad (1992) *The First Twenty-Five Years of the World Intellectual Property Organization from 1967 to 1992* (WIPO Publication No. 881 [E]) (Geneva, Switzerland: International Bureau of Intellectual Property).

Bogsch's own discussion of the history and politics of the WIPO. An indispensable source for understanding the politics behind the WIPO's mission.

Commission on Intellectual Property Rights (CIPR) (2002) *Integrating Intellectual Property Rights and Development Policy* (London: CIPR/Department for International Development).

This report has become a touchstone for those critical of the manner in which the global governance of intellectual property has developed in the last decade and as such is required reading for anyone interested in the global political economy of IPRs. Additionally it was a key element in the debates that preceded and informed the development of the proposed Development Agenda for the WIPO.

Correa, Carlos M. and Musungu, Sisule F. (2002) *The WIPO Patent Agenda: The Risks for Developing Countries* (T.R.A.D.E. working paper No. 12) (Geneva, Switzerland: South Centre).

An excellent overview of the Patent Agenda and its likely impact on developing countries by two of the leading commentators in the field.

Doern, G. Bruce (1999) *Global Change and Intellectual Property Agencies: An Institutional Perspective* (London: Pinter Publishers).

One of the few political economic analyses of the global governance of intellectual property to offer an account of the WIPO. Although now somewhat dated, Doern's analysis is still a useful and well informed contribution to the debates about the WIPO's future role in the global intellectual property system.

Drahos, Peter and Braithwaite, John (2002) *Information Feudalism: Who Owns the Knowledge Economy?* (London: Earthscan Publications).

An excellent overview of the political disputes about the global governance of IPRs in the last decade. Building on the authors' extensive research regarding the regulation of global business, this book explore the myriad disputes that led to the establishment of the TRIPs agreement. The authors also discuss the wide range of industrial sectors, and developmental issues that are affected by the enforcement of IPRs in the global political economy.

Matthews, Duncan (2002) *Globalizing Intellectual Property Rights: The TRIPs Agreement* (London: Routledge).

An excellent and comprehensive account of the global governance regime that was established by the TRIPs agreement.

May, Christopher and Sell, Susan (2005) *Intellectual Property Rights: A Critical History* (Boulder, Colo.: Lynne Rienner Publishers).

A wide ranging history of intellectual property that underpins many of the critical arguments made by NGOs and developing countries' representatives regarding the veracity of the claims made for intellectual property's benefits. This history establishes that IPRs can in no way be seen as "natural rights"; only by seeing IPRs as a key policy-driven social intervention can the contemporary problems that beset global governance be properly (historically) contextualized and understood.

Musungu, Sisule F. (2005) *Rethinking Innovation, Development and Intellectual Property in the UN: WIPO and Beyond* (TRIPS Issue Papers: 5) (Geneva, Switzerland: Quaker United Nations Office).

An excellent snap-shot of the progress of the discussion around the Development Agenda that sets out the various proposals in an easily accessible form and offers a well informed critique and evaluation of their various merits.

Musungu, Sisule F. and Dutfield, Graham (2003) *Multilateral Agreements and a TRIPs-Plus World: The World Intellectual Property Organization* (TRIPs Issue Papers: 3) (Geneva, Switzerland: Quaker United Nations Office).

A key political intervention examining the WIPO itself and making the key argument about the relationship with the United Nations that has subsequently been a major aspect of criticisms of the WIPO. This report (alongside Musungu's other work) firmly established the political context in which reforms of the WIPO can be understood and supported.

Index

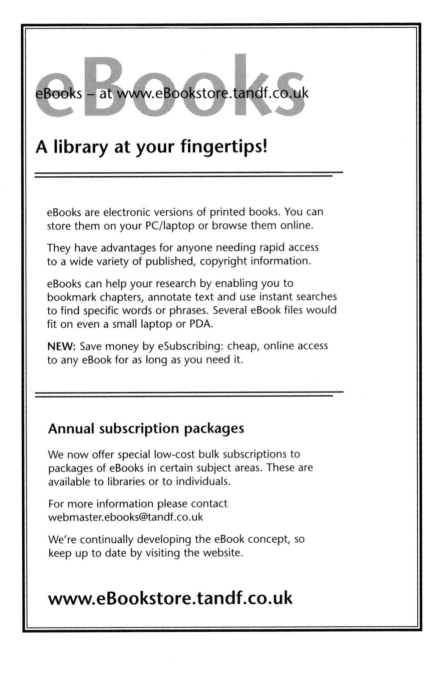